To

Diane

From

Judy

From My House to Yours

Also by John Hadamuscin

ENCHANTED EVENINGS
Dinners, Suppers, Picnics & Parties

SPECIAL OCCASIONS
Holiday Entertaining All Year Round

THE HOLIDAYS
Elegant Entertaining from Thanksgiving to Twelfth Night

JOHN HADAMUSCIN'S

From My House to Yours

Gifts, Recipes, and Remembrances from the Hearth and Home

Photographs by Randy O'Rourke

Harmony Books New York

DESIGNED BY KEN SANSONE

Published by Harmony Books, a division of Crown Publishers, Inc.,
201 East 50th Street, New York, New York 10022.
Member of the Crown Publishing Group.

HARMONY and colophon are trademarks of Crown Publishers, Inc.
Manufactured in Japan

LIBRARY OF CONGRESS CATALOGING-IN-PUBLICATION DATA

Hadamsucin, John.
From my house to yours:
gifts, recipes, and remembrances from the hearth and home/
John Hadamuscin; photographs by Randy O'Rourke.
p. cm.
Includes index.
1. Cookery. 2. Gifts. I. Title
TX652.H315 1990
641.5—dc20 90-27206
CIP

ISBN 0-517-58489-1

10 9 8 7 6 5 4 3 2 1

First Edition

A NOTE OF THANKS . . .

*to all those who have given so much
of themselves to me over the years.
They have taught me the process of receiving
and in turn taught me to be a better giver.*

Contents

AUTUMN

CHRISTMAS

Introduction

"A gift, though small, is welcome."
HOMER

A few years ago, when good friends moved into their new home, I made a huge wreath from grapevines and flowers and herbs I had dried as a housewarming gift. The wreath was immediately placed over the mantel, where it still hangs today. The colors may be a bit softer now, and the fragrances may have long since faded, but the wreath still stands as a symbol of our long friendship.

Last Christmas, I was in the usual quandary about what to give the adult members of my family (the kids are always easy!). Every year, as a little extra, I give everyone a jar of my Cranberry-Walnut Ketchup, so after much deliberation I finally decided to start with the ketchup and build from there. Everyone got big cellophane-wrapped and ribbon-tied baskets containing homemade gifts from my kitchen—the ketchup, of course, along with a figgy pudding, a tin of cookies, and a bottle of my holiday cordial. Tucked into each basket was a small treasure that personalized each one—a 1940s pie recipe booklet for my sister-in-law the baker, a compilation tape of Dixieland jazz for my brother the music lover, and so on. Well, I can't remember when my Christmas gifts were more enthusiastically received.

So, quite accidentally, I've started a tradition that my friends and family will look forward to as each new season comes along. Since I began practicing the old custom of giving gifts from my home, the ritual of giving for birthdays, Christmas, and other passages is no longer an obligation, but something I look forward to—giving is actually a joy, which is, after all, what it's supposed to be in the first place.

Whenever someone comes to visit, they invariably leave with a jar of something I've made, and when I go visiting, some little something goes along with me for my hosts. And whether a neighbor has just been elected to the school board or a friend just got a big promotion, whenever an occasion comes along where just a note would probably do, it seems a much nicer and more personal expression of caring and generosity to give even a small jar of marmalade or bundle of potpourri to commemorate the event.

In this little book, I've included some of my favorite gifts, those that I've given and some that I've received. The book is divided into what I consider to be the five gift-giving seasons of the year—Winter, Spring, Summer, Autumn *and*, right after fall and just before winter really sets in, the Christmas season. In each section, I've tried to make the gifts appropriate to the events of the season using currently available fruits, vegetables, herbs, and flowers from the garden.

The love, thought, and generosity displayed in the preparation are only part of a gift from the home—the presentation accounts for much of its appeal. I've included packaging ideas that are simple and require no special talents, and they can all be adapted for any gifts. These are only a few ideas to stimulate the imagination; feel free to be inventive and add your own touches.

And, remember—no matter what the gift or how it is presented, the act of giving comes from the heart. So, from my house to yours, and from your house to those near and dear to you, and on and on, best wishes and happy giving.

John

W I N T E R

For a Winter Afternoon

A Few Nice Things for Teatime

English Muffin Loaf
Apricot-Raisin Jam
Lime-Ginger Marmalade
Banana-Pecan Bread
Chocolate-Flecked Orange Tea Ring

It's a cold winter weekend and a good friend calls with an invitation to spend a lazy afternoon together, playing cards or the new board game and having tea. When you arrive with any of these treats in hand, you'll be an even more welcome guest.

"There are few hours in life more agreeable than the hours dedicated to the ceremony known as afternoon tea."
HENRY JAMES

English Muffin Loaf

Makes two 8½ × 4½-inch loaves

An easy yeast bread, this is great in all the same ways English muffins are used, especially toasted with butter and marmalade or jam. It makes wonderful grilled cheese sandwiches, too.

5½ to 6 cups unbleached all-purpose flour
2 envelopes active dry yeast
1 tablespoon sugar
1½ teaspoons salt
¼ teaspoon baking soda
2 cups milk, at room temperature
½ cup boiling water
Stoneground yellow cornmeal

1. Into a large mixing bowl, sift 3 cups of the flour. Add the yeast, sugar, salt, and soda and mix well. In a small separate bowl, combine the milk and water. Immediately pour the liquid mixture over the dry mixture and beat until the mixture is smooth. Add 2½ to 3 cups more flour, ½ cup at a time and beating after each addition, until a stiff batter is formed.

2. Butter two 8½ × 4½-inch loaf pans and sprinkle the bottoms and sides lightly with cornmeal. Divide the batter between the pans and lightly sprinkle the tops with cornmeal. Cover the pans with a damp, clean cloth, put in a warm, draft-free place, and allow the loaves to rise until doubled in bulk, 40 to 50 minutes.

3. Preheat the oven to 400°F. Place the pans in the oven and bake until the loaves are lightly browned and sound hollow when tapped lightly with a finger, about 30 minutes. Transfer the pans to a wire rack and allow to cool 5 minutes. Remove the loaves from the pans, place on the racks, and cool completely.

4. To serve, cut into ¼-inch-thick slices and toast in a toaster or under a preheated broiler.

◆ Wrap the loaves tightly in cellophane and tie with a red-white-and-blue ribbon. Include a small jar of homemade marmalade or jam with the gift.

Apricot-Raisin Jam

Makes about 4 half-pints

This is delicious with toasted thin slices of English Muffin Loaf (page 12). Dried apricots sold in bulk are usually more flavorful than the prepackaged kind; natural food stores are a good source.

½ pound dried apricot halves, coarsely chopped
1 cup golden raisins
Juice and grated rind of 1 lemon
1 cup orange juice
2 cups sugar

1. Place the apricots and raisins in a bowl and add water to cover. Cover the bowl tightly and let it stand overnight. Drain the liquid into a large, heavy saucepan and chop the apricots coarsely. Add the apricots, raisins, lemon juice and rind, and orange juice to the pan, place over low heat, and bring to a simmer. Cook 20 minutes, stirring occasionally.

2. Add the sugar and continue cooking, stirring frequently until the mixture of fruit is very soft and the syrup sheets when dropped from the side of a spoon (220°F. on a candy thermometer), 15 to 20 minutes. Spoon the jam into sterilized half-pint jars. Seal the jars, process in a boiling-water bath (page 50) for 10 minutes, and cool. Store in a cool, dark place.

Lime-Ginger Marmalade

Makes about 4 half-pints

3 to 4 limes halved lengthwise, sliced paper-thin crosswise, and seeded (enough to measure 1½ cups)
½ cup finely shredded lemon rind
5 cups water
¼ cup finely shredded gingerroot
4¼ cups sugar, approximately

1. Place all ingredients except the sugar in a heavy saucepan over medium-high heat. Bring the mixture to a boil and cook, boiling rapidly, for 30 minutes, or until the fruit is tender.

2. Measure the fruit mixture and for each cup of fruit add 1 cup of sugar. Return the mixture to a boil and continue cooking until the mixture sheets when dropped from the side of a spoon (220°F. on a candy thermometer), about 30 to 35 minutes.

3. Remove the pan from the heat and cool 5 minutes. Transfer the marmalade to four sterilized half-pint jars and seal. Store in a cool, dark place.

"One makes one's own happiness only by taking care of the happiness of others."
SAINT-PIERRE

Banana-Pecan Bread

Makes two 8 × 4½-inch loaves or four 5¾ × 3-inch loaves

Toasting the pecans gives this spicy bread an even more sumptuous flavor.

½ cup (1 stick) butter, softened
1 cup sugar
2 large eggs
1½ cups all-purpose flour
2 teaspoons baking powder
¼ teaspoon baking soda
½ teaspoon salt
1 teaspoon ground cinnamon
¼ teaspoon ground cloves
1½ cups mashed very ripe banana
1 teaspoon vanilla extract
¾ cup chopped pecans, lightly toasted (see page 71)

1. Preheat the oven to 350°F. Grease two 8 × 4½-inch or four 5¾ × 3-inch loaf pans.

2. In a mixing bowl, cream the butter and sugar together, then beat in the eggs. Into a separate bowl, sift together the flour, baking powder, baking soda, salt, cinnamon, and cloves. Add this dry mixture to the wet mixture and mix well, then beat in the banana and vanilla. Stir in the nuts.

3. Transfer the batter to the pan(s) and bake until the bread is nicely browned and a cake tester inserted in the center comes out clean, about 1 hour for the larger loaves and 50 minutes for the smaller ones. Remove the bread from the pan(s) and cool on a wire rack. Store, tightly wrapped, in a cool place.

Chocolate-flecked Orange Tea Ring

Makes one 10-inch round tube cake

1 cup (2 sticks) butter, softened
4 ounces cream cheese, softened
1¾ cups sugar
3 large eggs
Grated rind of 2 large oranges
2 cups all-purpose flour
1 teaspoon baking powder
⅔ cup coarsely grated semisweet chocolate

1. Preheat the oven to 375°F. Grease a 10-inch tube pan very well, line the bottom with wax paper, and grease the wax paper.

2. In a large mixing bowl, beat together the butter and cream cheese until well blended. Add the sugar, eggs, and orange rind and beat until the mixture is light and fluffy. Into a separate bowl, sift together the flour and baking powder, then beat this into the butter mixture until blended and smooth. Stir in the chocolate.

3. Transfer the batter to the prepared pan and bake for 40 to 45 minutes, or until the cake is a light golden brown and springs back when lightly pressed. Cool for 15 minutes in the pan, then remove from the pan. Place the cake on a wire rack to cool completely.

For Keeping Warm at Night

HOT SOUPS AND WARM DRINKS

Winter Tomato Soup
Galician Bean Soup
Butternut Squash and Apple Soup
Hot Mochaccino Mix
Mulled Drink Spice Bundles

"Drink plenty of warm liquids" is always comforting advice when a cold or flu, or even just the weather, gets us down. And soups and hot drinks always do make us feel better in the depths of winter. Soups are generally not thought of as gifts, but they're always appreciated, whether taken to the host of a ski weekend or even just next door as a surprise treat for a neighbor.

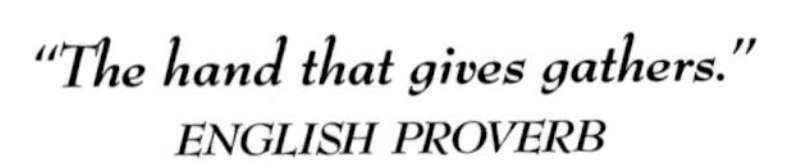

"The hand that gives gathers."
ENGLISH PROVERB

WINTER TOMATO SOUP

Makes about 3 quarts

3 tablespoons olive oil
¾ cup finely chopped celery
2 medium onions, finely chopped
4 large shallots, finely chopped
2 28-ounce cans Italian plum tomatoes
1 teaspoon dried basil
½ teaspoon dried oregano
½ teaspoon dried thyme
¼ cup chopped parsley
2 bay leaves
3 cups well-seasoned chicken stock
Salt and freshly ground black pepper

1. In a Dutch oven or large, heavy saucepan, combine the oil, celery, onion, and shallots and place over medium heat. Sauté until the vegetables are soft and golden, 7 to 10 minutes.

2. Add the tomatoes, crushing them against the side of the pan to break them into small pieces. Stir in the herbs and chicken stock and bring to a boil. Reduce the heat and simmer for 30 minutes. Season to taste with salt and plenty of pepper.

3. Ladle the soup into three sterilized 1-quart jars, leaving a ¼-inch space at the top. Seal the jars and process in a boiling-water bath (page 50) for 20 minutes. Cool the jars and store in a cool place.

Galician Bean Soup

Makes about 4 quarts

On a cold night, this hearty main course soup is good for whatever ails you.

- 2 cups dried white beans, picked over and rinsed
- ¼ pound slab bacon *or* lean salt pork, diced
- 3 large garlic cloves, finely chopped
- 3 medium onions, chopped
- 1 cup diced celery
- 1 cup diced carrots
- 3 quarts well-seasoned stock (chicken, veal, or turkey)
- ½ teaspoon salt
- 2 bay leaves
- ½ teaspoon dried marjoram
- 2 cups diced potatoes
- 3 cups coarsely shredded kale *or* cabbage
- ¼ cup chopped flat-leaf parsley
- Salt and freshly ground black pepper

1. Place the beans in a medium saucepan with water to cover by a few inches. Cover the pan, place over high heat, and bring to a boil. Turn off the heat and let stand 1 hour.

2. In a large, heavy stockpot or Dutch oven over medium heat, sauté the bacon until it browns and most of the fat is rendered. Remove the bacon with a slotted spoon and reserve. Remove all but about 3 tablespoons fat and reserve for another use. Add the garlic, onions, celery, and carrots and sauté until the vegetables are golden, about 10 minutes.

3. Drain the beans and add them to the stockpot, along with the reserved bacon, the stock, salt, bay leaves, and marjoram. Bring to a simmer and cook 20 minutes. Add the potatoes and simmer 20 minutes longer. Add the kale or cabbage and continue simmering until the beans and potatoes are tender, about 10 minutes longer. Stir in the parsley and season to taste with salt and fresh pepper.

4. To store, ladle the soup into 1- or 2-quart jars, let cool, and refrigerate. Reheat before serving.

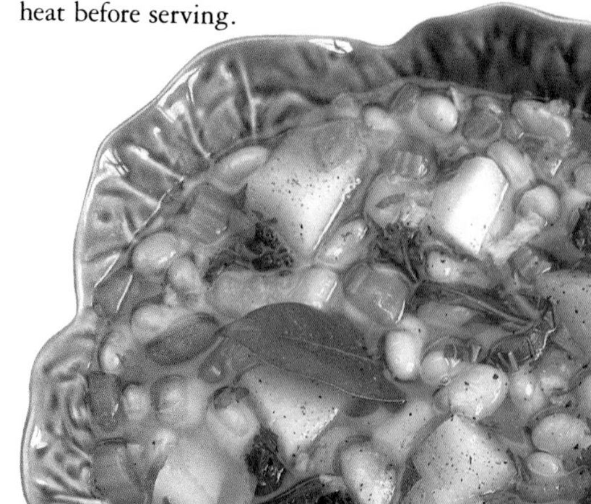

Butternut Squash and Apple Soup

Makes about 3 quarts

When I first tasted this soup, it was served as the first course at an elegant dinner, but I like serving it fireside, in mugs, as a warming accompaniment to ham or smoked turkey sandwiches on crusty black bread.

2 tablespoons butter
2 medium onions, coarsely chopped
1 large or 2 medium butternut squash (about 3 pounds), peeled, seeded, and cut into chunks
4 tart green apples, peeled, cored, and cut into chunks
2 large boiling potatoes, peeled and cut into chunks
6 cups well-seasoned chicken stock
¼ teaspoon dried rosemary, crumbled
¼ teaspoon dried marjoram, crumbled
Salt and freshly ground black pepper
Grated extra-sharp Cheddar or Parmesan

1. Melt the butter in a heavy stockpot or Dutch oven over medium-low heat. Add the onions and sauté until golden but not browned, about 15 minutes. Add the squash, apples, potatoes, stock, and herbs. Increase the heat and bring the mixture to a boil. Reduce the heat and simmer until the vegetables are very tender, about 30 minutes.

2. In batches, puree the soup until smooth in the bowl of a food processor fitted with the steel chopping blade. Return the soup to the pan and season to taste with salt and pepper. Serve hot and pass a small bowl of grated cheese.

3. To store, ladle the soup into 1-quart jars and store in the refrigerator up to 4 days.

Variations Substitute 4 teaspoons curry powder for the herbs and omit the cheese garnish. Serve either version of the soup cold rather than hot.

"Who would not give all else for two pennysworth of beautiful soup?"
LEWIS CARROLL

Hot Mochaccino Mix

Makes about 2¼ cups, enough for 10 to 12 servings

1 cup superfine sugar
⅔ cup unsweetened Dutch-process cocoa
1 teaspoon ground cinnamon
¼ teaspoon grated nutmeg
2 tablespoons instant espresso powder
½ cup nonfat dry milk

1. Combine all ingredients in a mixing bowl and blend well. Pack into small tins or bags.

2. For each serving, combine 3 to 4 tablespoons mix with ¾ cup milk in a small saucepan and bring to just below the simmering point, whisking until smooth and frothy. Serve hot in mugs. Add a dab of whipped cream and a grating of nutmeg, if you'd like.

◆ Pack the mix in a small decorative tin or a small brown paper bag tied with twine. When using old tins, pack the mix into small plastic bags and then pack a bag into each tin.

Mulled drink spice bundles in the making.

Mulled Drink Spice Bundles

Here's a quick and simple gift when you need one on the spur of the moment: Make small spice bundles, each containing 3 small cinnamon sticks broken in half, 2 teaspoons whole allspice, 2 teaspoons whole cloves, and 3 or 4 star anise; add a strip or two of dried citrus peel and 2 or 3 cardamom pods if you have them. Tie the ingredients up in 6-inch squares of cheesecloth with kitchen string.

Pack a few bundles in a small jar or tin to keep the spices fresh and tie it all up with ribbons. Or tie a single bundle onto the neck of a bottle of fresh cider or wine. In any case, include the following instructions for using the bundles:

In a small kettle, combine 2 quarts cider, cranberry juice, white or light red wine (individually or in any combination) with 1 spice bundle (remove ribbons first!) and 1 thinly sliced orange or lemon and place over low heat. Slowly bring the mixture to just below the simmering point. Keep the mixture on the stove at this temperature for 20 minutes or so, allowing the flavors to blend. Ladle into mugs and serve warm.

Dinner for Two

FOR VALENTINE'S DAY

Fettuccine with Prosciutto, Walnuts, Wild Mushrooms, and Sage
Green Salad
Iced Tangerines in Cassis
Chocolate Sugar Hearts

There are some annual events that tend to be more gift-worthy than others. Even so, on Valentine's Day it's become something of a tradition (or maybe just a bad habit) to merely stop on the way home at the end of the day to pick up a box of candy or a bunch of flowers. The idea here, in contrast, is to show up with a handwritten "gift certificate" for dinner for two, along with a sackful of the ingredients, and then to cook it up pronto.

The simple dinner consists of a quick and sensuous pasta dish accompanied by a simple green salad, followed by icy tangerines in cassis (prepare these first) and made-ahead chocolate sugar hearts. With a little organization, preparation should take no more than half an hour.

Fettuccine with Prosciutto, Walnuts, Wild Mushrooms, and Sage

Serves 2

This is a rather heady combination—complex in flavor but quick and easy to make.

½ pound fettuccine (whole wheat, spinach, or a combination)
2 tablespoons extra-virgin olive oil
2 shallots, finely chopped
¼ pound shiitake mushrooms, thinly sliced
¼ cup coarsely chopped walnuts
¼ pound thinly sliced prosciutto, cut into ¼-inch strips
2 tablespoons chopped sage leaves (see note)
2 tablespoons butter, softened
1 cup half-and-half
¼ cup grated Parmesan cheese
Whole sage leaves, for garnish

1. Heat the oil in a large skillet or Dutch oven over medium heat. Add the shallots, mushrooms, and 2 tablespoons walnuts, and sauté until the shallots are transparent and the mushrooms are golden brown, 8 to 10 minutes. Stir in the prosciutto and chopped sage and remove from the heat.

2. Meanwhile, bring a kettle of salted water to a boil. Add the fettuccine and cook until *al dente* (the timing will depend on whether the pasta is fresh or dried, its thickness, etc.). While the fettuccine is cooking, whisk the butter, half-and-half, and cheese into the skillet.

3. Immediately after draining the pasta, return it to the kettle, add the skillet mixture, and toss well. Season with salt and plenty of fresh pepper. Serve immediately, garnished with whole sage leaves and the remaining chopped walnuts.

NOTE If fresh sage is absolutely unavailable, substitute ½ teaspoon dried sage.

Simple Green Salad

With this intensely flavored main course, a simple salad seems best. A wide variety of salad greens are now available year-round; for two, use a head of Boston lettuce or 2 cups of leaf lettuce (red or green, or a combination), torn into bite-size pieces. To dress the salad, whisk together ¼ cup olive oil, 1½ tablespoons vinegar (balsamic, sherry, or red wine), and ½ teaspoon Dijon mustard and add a pinch of salt and a grind or two of black pepper.

"Kissin' don't last, but cookin' do!"
OLD SAYING

Iced Tangerines in Cassis

Serves 2

A refreshing dessert after a rich dinner.

¼ cup crème de cassis liqueur
2 tablespoons sugar
6 whole cloves
4 star anise (optional)
3 tangerines, peeled, cut crosswise into thin slices, and seeded

1. Combine the cassis, sugar, cloves, and star anise in a small, heavy saucepan over medium heat. Bring to a simmer and cook until syrupy, about 5 minutes. Remove from the heat and allow to cool.

2. Place the tangerine slices in a shallow bowl and pour the syrup over them. Cover and refrigerate for an hour or so. *(Can be made up to a day before serving.)* Place the tangerines in the freezer for 20 minutes before serving so they're icy cold.

Chocolate Sugar Hearts

Makes 2 to 3 dozen cookies, depending on the size of the cutters

5 ounces unsweetened chocolate
5 ounces semisweet chocolate
¼ cup (½ stick) butter
½ cup granulated sugar

½ cup firmly packed dark brown sugar
2 large eggs
2 teaspoons vanilla extract
1 cup all-purpose flour
½ teaspoon baking soda
½ teaspoon ground cinnamon
½ teaspoon salt
1 tablespoon milk
Sugar for sprinkling

1. Combine the chocolates and butter in a large, heavy saucepan and place over very low heat until melted. Remove from the heat and gradually stir in the sugars. Beat 1 egg lightly; stir it into the chocolate mixture, then stir in the vanilla.

2. In a mixing bowl, sift together the flour, baking soda, cinnamon, and salt. Gradually stir this into the melted chocolate mixture, stirring until well blended. Form the dough into a ball, wrap with wax paper, and chill for half an hour.

3. Preheat the oven to 375°F. Lightly grease baking sheets.

4. Roll the dough out between two sheets of wax paper to a thickness of about ⅛ inch. Use a heart-shaped cookie cutter to cut out the cookies, and place them on the baking sheets. Beat the remaining egg with the 1 tablespoon milk. Brush the surface of the dough with the beaten egg mixture and sprinkle liberally with sugar.

5. Bake until the edges are browned, about 12 minutes. Cool the cookies on the pan for 5 minutes, then remove to wire racks to cool completely. Pack into a tightly covered container and store in a cool, dry place.

◆ For giving, pack the cookies into a fancy heart-shaped candy box lined with white paper doilies. Tie up the box with red or gold satin or lace ribbons and tuck a rose into the bow at the last minute.

S P R I N G

Blossom Time

GIFTS FROM THE GARDEN AND FOR THE GARDENER

A basket of spring's first hyacinths.

Once I see the first forsythia branches spotted with little specks of green and yellow (and I've been known to literally force the issue by bringing the branches inside and putting them in warm water), spring fever takes over. And as spring rolls along, I've got flowers—from a single peony in an old green vinegar bottle to a big varied bouquet tucked into a basket—all over the house. Since everyone loves flowers just as much as I do, when it comes to gift-giving they're a natural.

Left: Tulips in an old dimestore vase. Below: A primrose plant in a basket and a fabric-wrapped hydrangea.

Gifts for the Garden(er)

- An antique or other unusual variety of rosebush
- A collection of potted herb plants
- A seedling fruit tree
- New gadgets for gardening
- For the city gardener, a window box—plants and all
- A beautiful and informative gardening book
- A subscription to a favorite gardening magazine
- In late spring, a few tomato plants
- A handcrafted or antique vase
- A gift certificate for a favorite gardening catalog or a nursery
- In fall, bulbs for sprouting in spring
- An outrageous garden ornament
- A handmade birdhouse
- A certificate volunteering X man-hours in the recipient's garden
- A stack of seed catalogs and a check
- A few garden gifts packed into an earthenware pot or planter

Thinking Pink

RHUBARB AND STRAWBERRIES

Strawberry Bread
Gingery Rhubarb Crisp
Strawberry-Rhubarb Coffee Cake
Tutti-frutti Strawberry Jam

"Friendship consists in forgetting what one gives and remembering what one receives."
DUMAS THE YOUNGER

By the time May and June roll around I'm itching for fruity desserts and I start "thinking pink." Rhubarb and strawberries are the first fruits to appear on the scene (even though rhubarb isn't a fruit at all), and when they do, I start planning what I'm going to do with them. Maybe the season's greatest gift of all is a dish of perfect strawberries with a drizzle of cream, but I'm always willing to consider these alternatives.

Strawberry Bread

Makes two 8½ × 4½-inch loaves

This is an unusual fruit quick bread, in that it has no added spices, allowing the strawberries themselves to shine. Its flavor and texture are best a day after it's baked. The bread is delicious toasted and lightly buttered for breakfast or toasted and topped with homemade strawberry ice cream for a late-night snack.

P.S. This bread freezes well for up to a month, so it's a good one to keep on hand when you need a quick gift.

- 4 large eggs
- 1 cup vegetable oil
- 2 cups sugar
- 3 cups all-purpose flour
- 1 teaspoon baking soda
- ½ teaspoon salt
- 3 cups strawberries, hulled and thinly sliced
- 1 teaspoon grated orange rind

1. Preheat the oven to 350°F. Generously grease two 8½ × 4½-inch nonstick loaf pans (if pans are not nonstick, grease them, line the bottoms with wax paper, and grease the wax paper).

2. In a mixing bowl, beat the eggs until light and fluffy, then beat in the oil until blended. Beat in the sugar. In a separate bowl, sift together the flour, baking soda, and salt.

3. Beat all but about 2 tablespoons of the dry mixture into the egg-oil mixture. Add the strawberries to the remaining dry mixture and toss to coat the berries well. Fold this mixture and the orange rind into the batter.

4. Divide the batter between the two prepared pans. Bake until the loaves are nicely browned and a cake tester inserted in the center comes out clean, 60 to 70 minutes. Transfer the pans to wire racks and cool 30 minutes. Run a knife around the edges of the pans and carefully remove the loaves. Return the loaves to the racks to cool completely.

◆ Wrap the loaves in plastic wrap or cellophane and tie up with ribbon.

Gingery Rhubarb Crisp

Serves 6 to 8

FILLING

8 cups diced rhubarb (about 3 pounds)
2 tablespoons finely chopped gingerroot
½ cup granulated sugar
3 tablespoons cornstarch
Juice and grated rind of 1 orange

TOPPING

1½ cups coarsely crushed store-bought gingersnaps
1 cup quick-cooking oats
¼ cup firmly packed dark brown sugar
1 teaspoon ground cinnamon
½ teaspoon ground ginger
¾ cup (1½ sticks) cold butter, cut into small pieces
½ cup sliced almonds
1 large egg, lightly beaten

1. Preheat the oven to 350°F. Butter a 9½-inch deep-dish pie pan or shallow 2½- to 3-quart baking dish.

2. In a mixing bowl, combine all the filling ingredients. Transfer the filling to the prepared pan and wipe out the bowl.

3. In the bowl, combine the cookie crumbs, oats, brown sugar, and spices. Using a pastry blender or two knives, cut in the butter. Add the almonds and the egg and toss the mixture lightly until just blended. Spread the topping evenly over the filling.

4. Bake the crisp until the filling is bubbly and the topping is well browned, about 45 minutes. Serve warm, or cool, cover, and refrigerate.

Strawberry-Rhubarb Coffee Cake

Makes one 9-inch square cake

2 cups sifted all-purpose flour
¼ cup granulated sugar
3 teaspoons baking powder
1 teaspoon salt
⅓ cup vegetable shortening
1 cup milk
1 large egg
1 cup thinly sliced rhubarb
1 cup sliced strawberries
¼ cup (½ stick) butter
½ cup firmly packed light brown sugar
¼ teaspoon ground ginger
¼ teaspoon ground cinnamon

1. Preheat the oven to 400°F. Grease a 9-inch square baking pan.

"The truly generous is the truly wise."
JOHN HOME

2. Sift together the flour, granulated sugar, baking powder, and salt into a mixing bowl. Cut in the shortening until the mixture resembles coarse meal. In a separate bowl, beat the milk and egg together with a fork to blend. Add the wet mixture to the dry mixture and stir quickly to form a soft dough.

3. Spread the dough evenly in the prepared pan and scatter the rhubarb and then the strawberries over it in an even layer. In a mixing bowl, cream together the butter, brown sugar, and spices, then spread this mixture evenly over the fruit.

4. Bake until the edges of the cake are lightly browned and a cake tester comes out clean, about 40 minutes. Cool the cake in the pan.

◆ Cut the cake into 3-inch squares, pack into a napkin-lined, small, shallow basket. Wrap in cellophane and tie up with a ribbon.

Tutti-frutti Strawberry Jam

Makes about 8 half-pints

- 1 small orange, quartered and seeded
- 1 small lemon, quartered and seeded
- 3 pints strawberries, washed and hulled
- 2 8-ounce cans crushed pineapple in juice, drained
- 1 cup golden raisins
- 8 cups sugar

1. Place the orange and lemon in the bowl of a food processor fitted with the steel blade and process until very coarsely chopped. Add the berries and continue processing until the berries are coarsely chopped.

2. Transfer the fruit to a large, heavy saucepan and stir in the pineapple, raisins, and sugar. Place the pan over medium-high heat and bring the mixture to a simmer, stirring frequently. Reduce the heat and simmer until the liquid sheets when dropped from the side of a spoon (220°F. on a candy thermometer), 20 to 25 minutes.

3. Spoon the preserves into 8 sterilized half-pint canning jars, leaving a ¼-inch space at the top. Seal the jars and process in a boiling-water bath (see page 50) for 10 minutes. Store the jars in a cool, dark place.

Breakfast in Bed

FOR MOTHER'S OR FATHER'S DAY

Cornmeal Flapjacks
Maple-Walnut Muffins
Raisin-Gingerbread Muffins

On Mother's Day and Father's Day, we always fixed breakfast for the honored parent (and served it to them whether they were awake and ready yet or not!) and I know it's a tradition in a lot of other homes as well. Here are a couple of recipes that are easy enough for kids to make themselves (with maybe just a little supervision). Breakfast can be rounded out with fresh fruit and a pot of freshly brewed coffee.

These recipes don't have to be limited to breakfast in bed either—as a gift, homemade muffins or flapjacks mix will be welcomed by just about anyone, day or night.

CORNMEAL FLAPJACK MIX

Makes 4 cups, enough for about 2 dozen pancakes

1½ cups stone-ground yellow cornmeal
2½ cups all-purpose flour
4 teaspoons baking powder
¼ cup sugar
1 teaspoon salt
⅛ teaspoon grated nutmeg
¼ cup shortening

Into a mixing bowl, sift together the cornmeal, flour, baking powder, sugar, salt, and nutmeg. Cut in the shortening. Store in a tightly covered container in a cool place.

◆ Pack in a tightly sealed small brown paper bag tied with twine. Include instructions for mixing the batter right on the bag.

CORNMEAL FLAPJACKS

Makes 6 to 8

1⅓ cups cornmeal flapjack mix (preceding recipe)
1 lightly beaten egg
⅔ cup milk

1. Preheat the griddle. In a mixing bowl, combine the ingredients and beat lightly with a fork to just moisten the dry ingredients—the batter will be lumpy.

2. For each flapjack, drop a few tablespoonfuls of batter onto the hot griddle. When small bubbles appear at the edges of the pancakes and the edges are lightly browned, flip the flapjacks over and cook the other side. Serve hot.

Maple-Walnut Muffins

Makes 1 dozen muffins

1 cup whole-wheat flour
1 cup sifted all-purpose flour
3 tablespoons sugar
½ teaspoon salt
1 tablespoon baking powder
¼ cup vegetable shortening
1 egg
½ cup milk
½ cup maple syrup
1 cup chopped walnuts

1. Preheat the oven to 400°F. Lightly grease a 12-cup muffin pan.

2. Into a mixing bowl, sift together the flours, sugar, salt, and baking powder. Using a pastry blender or two knives, cut in the shortening. In a separate bowl, mix the egg, milk, and syrup until blended. Add to the dry mixture and stir quickly with a fork to just moisten—do not overmix. Stir in the nuts.

3. Fill the cups of the muffin pan about two-thirds full and bake until the edges are browned, 20 to 25 minutes. Serve hot, or cool on a wire rack and store in a tightly covered container in a cool place.

Raisin-Gingerbread Muffins Add 1 teaspoon ground cinnamon and 1½ teaspoons ground ginger to the dry ingredients in step 1. Substitute dark molasses for the maple syrup and 1 cup golden raisins for the walnuts.

S U M M E R

"Thanks for a Great Weekend"

Gifts from Guest to Host

Stilton-Walnut Savories
Mushroom Tapenade
Bourbon Barbecue Sauce
Tomato Chutney
Early Summer Floral Potpourri
Midsummer Herbal Potpourri

In my experience as both a weekend host and a weekend guest, I've found that the gifts most often appreciated are things that the host can actually use—both for his own enjoyment and that of his guests. I, and just about any host, will always welcome the little package that helps make the weekend afternoon cocktail hour or dinnertime a bit easier, or a little bundle that brings the smells of summer indoors. (Of course, if anyone wants to bring me an antique or a handcrafted Santa Claus, no matter what the season, come on over!) So here are a few of my favorite host and hostess gifts, some that I've both given and received.

Stilton-Walnut Savories

Makes about 5 dozen crackers

Every host is always happy to have a nibble or two on hand to serve during the cocktail hour (which on lazy summer afternoons tends to start earlier and last longer than in winter months), and these crackers are always well received.

- ½ cup (1 stick) butter
- ¼ pound Stilton cheese, finely crumbled
- 1 cup all-purpose flour
- ¼ teaspoon salt
- ½ cup finely chopped walnuts

1. Combine the butter and cheese in a large bowl and mix well. Gradually blend in the flour and salt, then blend in the nuts. Form the dough into a ball, wrap well, and refrigerate for 2 or 3 hours.

2. Preheat the oven to 350°F. Lightly grease baking sheets. Remove the dough from the refrigerator and unwrap it. Roll it out into a circle slightly less than ¼ inch thick. Cut the dough into 1½-inch squares and cut each square diagonally in half.

3. Place the triangles on the baking sheets, prick well with a fork, and bake until the crackers are lightly browned, 10 to 12 minutes. Cool the crackers on wire racks and pack into wax paper–lined tins, tightly covered.

Mushroom Tapenade

Makes about 3 half-pints

Any host will welcome this quick fix for cocktail time. It's equally good lightly spread onto toasted thin slices of baguette or used as a hearty dip for raw summer vegetables.

½ pound shiitake or other "wild" mushrooms, finely chopped
12 ounces button mushrooms, finely chopped
2 large garlic cloves, crushed
½ cup extra-virgin olive oil
4 scallions, white and green parts, coarsely chopped
1 cup drained and pitted oil-cured black olives
2 teaspoons thyme leaves *or* ½ teaspoon dried thyme
½ cup loosely packed flat-leaf parsley
Juice of 1 lemon
3 tablespoons drained capers
Freshly ground black pepper

1. Combine the mushrooms, garlic, and 3 tablespoons of the oil in a heavy skillet and place over medium heat. Sauté the mushrooms until they have released all their liquid and it's cooked away and the mushrooms are dark brown. Remove from the heat and cool.

2. Pour the remaining oil into the bowl of a food processor fitted with the steel chopping blade (reserve the mushrooms). Add the scallions, olives, thyme, parsley, and lemon juice and process until smooth. Add the mushrooms and process until just blended in. Stir in the capers and season with plenty of black pepper.

3. Transfer the tapenade to half-pint jars or crocks, cover tightly, and store in the refrigerator.

Bourbon Barbecue Sauce

Makes about 3 half-pints

This non-tomato barbecue sauce is a welcome gift for any summer weekend host. It's especially good on chicken and pork that have perhaps been marinated in a little orange juice, olive oil, and garlic (the sauce should be liberally brushed on during the last few minutes of grilling). Equally good are shrimp and scallops that have been marinated in the sauce for an hour or so, skewered, and then quickly grilled.

½ cup (1 stick) butter
6 medium onions, finely chopped
6 large garlic cloves, finely chopped
1½ cups Bourbon whiskey
1½ cups cider vinegar
Juice of 2 lemons
½ cup light molasses
⅛ teaspoon cayenne pepper (or more to taste)
1 tablespoon dry mustard
3 6-ounce cans frozen orange juice concentrate, thawed

1. In a medium, heavy, nonreactive saucepan, melt the butter over medium heat. Add the onions and garlic and sauté until soft and golden, about 7 minutes.

2. Add all the remaining ingredients except the orange juice concentrate and stir until smooth. Bring to a simmer, stirring occasionally. Turn the heat down to low and continue to simmer, uncovered, until the mixture is thick, about 45 minutes. Stir in the orange juice concentrate and bring to a simmer again.

3. Transfer the sauce to 3 sterilized half-pint jars, leaving a ⅛-inch space at the top of the jars. Process in a boiling-water bath (see page 50) for 10 minutes. Cool, label, and store in a cool, dark place.

◆ Cover the jar lids with small squares of red gingham or squares cut from bandanas, tied on with brown twine.

A Few Welcome Gifts for the Summer Weekend Host

- Antique linen hand towels
- A tin of tea or a bag of coffee beans and a pair of handmade mugs
- Hand-dipped candles and maybe a pair of Depression glass candlesticks
- A bottle of dessert wine
- The latest "hot" board game
- An old-fashioned screen flyswatter!

Tomato Chutney

Makes 6 half-pints

When I'm hosting for a weekend, I'm frequently looking for an easy way out when lunchtime arrives and I've gotten myself involved in some other project. Chutneys and relishes can help jazz up a simple lunch of bread and cheese and cold meats, so they're always nice to have on hand. This is especially good with sliced roasted or grilled lamb, beef, or pork.

3 cups sugar
2 cups red wine vinegar
3 large cloves garlic, minced
1 teaspoon salt
¾ teaspoon hot red pepper flakes
1 teaspoon ground ginger
4 pounds firm, slightly underripe medium tomatoes, cut into eighths

1. In a medium, heavy saucepan over medium heat, combine all the ingredients except the tomatoes. Bring to a boil, reduce the heat, and simmer, uncovered, for 25 minutes.

2. Add the tomatoes and continue simmering gently until the tomatoes are just softened and the liquid is thick and syrupy, about 15 minutes. Transfer the chutney to 6 sterilized half-pint jars and seal. Process in a boiling-water bath (page 50) for 10 minutes, cool, and store in a cool, dark place.

Potpourri—A Basic Recipe

Makes about 8 cups

The ingredients lists below are only suggestions—choose any combination, based on availability and your own preferences (all measurements are for *dried* leaves and flowers; see step 1). The only essential is the orris root, available at herbal or floral supply shops, which helps preserve the scents of the ingredients. A few drops of a compatible essential oil can be added when making the potpourri or later on to refresh its aroma.

1. Using the list below as a guide, gather perfect, unbruised flowers and leaves. Arrange the leaves, flower petals, and stemmed small whole flowers in a single layer on an old screen or a drying tray (tulle fabric stretched across a wood frame will do as a homemade drying tray) in a warm, dry, not-too-well-lit place, and let stand until they are dried and brittle (timing will depend on the humidity in the air and the moisture content of the leaves and flowers themselves).

2. If the leaves and flowers are not being used immediately, carefully pack each variety separately in jars (old 2-quart mayonnaise jars work well), label, and store in a dark, dry place.

3. Select a combination of flowers and leaves, some for color and some for aroma, and combine them in a large glass or ceramic bowl. Add 1 teaspoon powdered orris root for every 4 cups of flowers and leaves. Add spices (see below) and a few drops of essential oil and gently toss the potpourri with your hands so as not to crush any flowers or leaves.

4. Transfer to large jars or other airtight containers (not metal tins) and store in a cool, dry, dark place for a week or so to allow the scents to mingle and mellow.

◆ Package potpourri in small cellophane bags, seal with kitchen string or

More potpourri blends for different seasons, left to right: An autumn blend of dried apple slices and orange rind, coxcomb, purple statice, white clover, thistles, Chinese lanterns, starbursts, marigolds, nuts, wheat, and bay leaves.

A holiday mixture of rose petals, pine needles and cones, bitterberries, orange and lime rind, eucalyptus, cinnamon sticks, whole allspice, and cloves.

A floral blend of rose petals, small whole roses, hyacinth blossoms, clover blossoms, nasturtium blossoms, lavender, and eucalyptus leaves.

wire twist-ties, and tie with pretty ribbons. Or make small sachets using lace-trimmed handkerchiefs, old printed hankies, or pinked squares of pretty fabric; tie up with kitchen string and cover the string with satin or lacy ribbons.

EARLY SUMMER FLORAL POTPOURRI

- 3 cups peony petals
- 2 cups rose petals and/or tiny whole roses
- 2 cups fruit blossoms
- ½ cup chamomile flowers and/or leaves
- ½ cup lavender leaves
- 1 tablespoon whole allspice

MIDSUMMER HERBAL POTPOURRI

- 2 cups rosemary flowers and leaves
- 2 cups rose geranium leaves and petals
- 1½ cups lemon thyme leaves
- ½ cup mint leaves
- ½ cup lavender leaves
- ½ cup woodruff
- 1 cup clover blossoms and/or bachelor buttons
- Thin strips of lime peel

From the Summer Bakery

A Few Good Desserts

A lot of my city friends think it's a heck of a lot of fun to go out to the country to pick their own berries. Well, back on the farm when we kids were called into service out in the fields, we didn't think it was much fun at all. But ultimately, Mom would bake a wonderful cake, or a pie, or a cobbler for dessert, and a day in the hot sun would be forgotten and forgiven. Here are a few summertime desserts that should make anyone happy at the beginning, middle, or end of a long hot summer day.

Summer Squash Tea Cake

Makes one 10-inch tube or bundt cake

This cake is a nice treat served on a shady porch or under a tree on a summer afternoon, accompanied by a big pitcher of iced tea. It's best when made a day in advance to allow the flavors to mellow.

- 2 cups grated yellow summer squash *or* zucchini (see note)
- 1 teaspoon salt
- ¾ cup granulated sugar
- 3 large eggs, at room temperature
- ⅞ cup vegetable oil
- ½ cup honey
- Juice and grated rind of 2 lemons
- 2½ cups all-purpose flour
- 2 teaspoons baking soda
- ½ teaspoon baking powder
- 1½ cups chopped pecans *or* almonds, lightly toasted (see page 71)
- Confectioners' sugar, for dusting

1. Place the squash in a colander and toss with the salt. Place a heavy plate or flat-bottomed bowl over the squash to weight it down, and let drain for 1 hour.

2. Preheat the oven to 350°F. Grease a 10-inch round tube or bundt pan.

3. In a mixing bowl, beat together the granulated sugar, eggs, oil, honey, and lemon juice and rind until well blended. Into a separate bowl, sift together the flour, baking soda, and baking powder.

Beat the dry mixture into the wet mixture until the batter is smooth. Squeeze any excess moisture from the squash, then stir the squash and the nuts into the batter.

4. Pour the batter into the prepared pan. Bake until lightly browned and a cake tester or toothpick inserted into the cake comes out clean, 35 to 40 minutes. Remove the pan to a wire rack and let cool 5 minutes, then invert the cake onto the rack to cool completely. Dust the cake lightly with confectioners' sugar.

NOTE The skin of yellow squash makes pretty speckles in the cake, so I leave it unpeeled. If you're substituting zucchini, you may want to peel it.

SQUASH TEA CAKE WITH CURRANTS Stir 1 cup fresh currants into the batter at the end of step 3.

◆ Place the cake on a paper doily-covered cutout circle of cardboard and place the cardboard on a large square of cellophane. Pull up the corners and sides so as not to touch the top of the cake and fasten them with a wire twist-tie or a rubber band. Tie up with a wide ribbon.

"It is not the shilling I give you that counts, but the warmth that is carried with it from my hand."

MIGUEL DE UNAMUNO

SUMMER FRUIT BARS

Makes about 3 dozen

CRUST

- ⅔ cup (1⅓ sticks) butter
- 1 3-ounce package cream cheese, softened
- ¼ cup firmly packed dark brown sugar
- 1 large egg
- 1 teaspoon vanilla extract
- 2 cups all-purpose flour
- ¼ teaspoon salt

FILLING

- ⅓ cup sugar
- 2 tablespoons all-purpose flour
- 1 teaspoon ground cinnamon
- ¼ teaspoon grated nutmeg
- 8 cups sliced fruit (nectarines, peaches, plums, or pitted and halved cherries)

TOPPING

- 1 cup all-purpose flour
- ¾ cup firmly packed dark brown sugar
- 1 tablespoon ground cinnamon
- ½ cup (1 stick) cold butter

1. Preheat the oven to 375°F. Lightly grease a jelly roll pan (approximately 10½ × 15-inches).

2. For the crust, cream the butter, cream cheese, and brown sugar together in a mixing bowl, then beat in the egg and the vanilla. Stir in the flour and salt until just blended in. Press the dough into the pan in an even layer.

3. For the filling, mix the sugar, flour, and spices in a small bowl, then toss this mixture with the fruit. Arrange the fruit in an even layer over the dough.

4. For the topping, combine the flour, brown sugar, and cinnamon in a small bowl. Cut in the butter until coarse crumbs are formed. Sprinkle the crumbs evenly over the fruit.

5. Bake for about 40 minutes, or until the fruit is tender and the topping is nicely browned. Cool in the pan on a wire rack and cut into 1½ × 3-inch bars. Cover and store in a cool place.

Peach and Almond Kuchen

Makes one 10-inch round cake

Whenever I go to tag sales, I'm always on the lookout for old Glassbake or Pyrex pie pans (they appear often at sales), so I've got plenty on hand to include as part of the gift with cakes like this one.

CAKE

- 1¼ cups unsifted all-purpose flour
- ½ cup sugar
- 1¾ teaspoons baking powder
- ½ teaspoon salt
- ¼ cup (½ stick) butter
- 1 large egg
- ½ cup milk
- 1 teaspoon vanilla extract

TOPPING

- 6 medium, firm, ripe peaches, peeled, pitted, and thinly sliced
- ¼ cup sliced almonds, lightly toasted (see page 71)
- ½ cup sugar
- ½ teaspoon ground cinnamon
- 1 teaspoon cornstarch
- ½ teaspoon almond extract
- ¼ cup (½ stick) butter, melted

1. Preheat the oven to 350°F. Lightly grease an ovenproof glass or ceramic 10-inch pie pan.

2. Combine the flour, ½ cup sugar, baking powder, and salt in a mixing bowl, then cut in the butter with a pastry blender or two knives. In a separate bowl, beat together the egg, milk, and vanilla, then stir this mixture into the dry mixture until just moistened.

3. Pour the batter into the prepared pan and arrange the peach slices in a spiral pattern over the batter. Scatter the almonds over the peaches. Combine the 1 cup sugar, cinnamon, and cornstarch and sprinkle this mixture over the peaches. Stir the almond extract into the melted butter and drizzle this mixture over all.

4. Bake for 30 to 35 minutes, or until the cake is lightly browned and a toothpick or cake tester comes out clean. Remove the cake from the oven and cool in the pan on a wire rack.

Any-Fruit Cobbler

Serves 6 to 8

When you're invited for dinner and volunteer to take dessert, an easy cobbler won't keep you in the kitchen very long. Just to add insult to injury, take along a pint of rich vanilla ice cream for topping the cobbler.

FILLING

- 6 cups fruit (see suggestions below)
- 1 tablespoon lemon juice
- 1 cup sugar
- 1 teaspoon ground cinnamon

TOPPING

- 1¾ cups sifted all-purpose flour
- 1 tablespoon sugar
- 1 tablespoon baking powder
- ½ teaspoon salt
- 6 tablespoons cold butter
- ⅞ cup milk
- 1 egg, lightly beaten with 1 tablespoon milk

1. Preheat the oven to 375°F. Grease a shallow, round 2-quart baking dish or a 9½-inch deep-dish pie pan, preferably ovenproof glass or earthenware. Place the fruit, lemon juice, 1 cup sugar, and cinnamon in the baking dish and toss well.

2. To make the topping, sift together the flour, 1 tablespoon sugar, baking powder, and salt and then cut in the butter with a pastry blender or two knives until the mixture is the consistency of coarse meal. Add the milk and beat with a fork until the milk is just blended in, forming a stiff, sticky dough.

3. Drop the dough by tablespoonfuls onto the fruit, leaving a few spaces between the dough drops for the fruit to bubble up. Brush the surface of the dough with the beaten egg mixture and bake until the fruit is bubbly and the top is golden brown, 30 to 35 minutes. Serve warm or at room temperature.

SUGGESTED FRUITS AND COMBINATIONS 6 cups sliced Italian purple plums, peaches, or nectarines; 2 pints blueberries and 2 cups sliced firm, ripe bananas; 4 cups sliced peaches and 1 pint raspberries or blackberries; 3 cups sliced strawberries and 3 cups sliced apples.

GLAZED BERRY TARTLETS

Makes 1 dozen

I like mixing a variety of berries—blueberries, strawberries, blackberries, or raspberries—but individual tartlets can each be made with a single type. Other fruits can be used as well: seedless red and green grapes, sliced peaches, plums, nectarines, or kiwis.

The shells can be baked a day in advance, but it's best to assemble the tartlets no more than a few hours before serving.

PASTRY SHELLS

¼ cup (½ stick) butter, softened
¼ cup vegetable shortening
¼ cup sugar
¼ teaspoon salt
1 teaspoon grated lemon rind
1 large egg, separated
1½ cups sifted all-purpose flour

FILLING

3 cups assorted berries, approximately, washed and well dried
½ cup currant jelly, melted

1. Make the pastry by combining the butter, shortening, sugar, salt, lemon rind, and egg white together in a mixing bowl and blending until smooth. Gradually blend in the flour to form a soft dough.

2. Press the dough evenly into 3-inch tartlet tins and brush lightly with the egg yolk. Place the tins on a baking sheet, cover with wax paper or aluminum foil, and chill in refrigerator for 30 minutes.

3. Preheat the oven to 375°F., then bake the tartlet shells until golden brown, 10 to 12 minutes. Cool the shells in the tins for 5 minutes, then remove to a wire rack to cool completely.

4. Fill each shell with a mound of about ¼ cup berries, then, using a small pastry brush, glaze the berries generously with the melted jelly, covering the surface completely. Keep in a cool place until serving (it's best not to refrigerate).

◆ Pack and transport tartlets in a covered pie basket lined with a checked tea towel or napkin; or use a shirt- or sweater-sized gift box.

The Last Gifts of Summer

PICKLING AND PRESERVING

Berry Vinegar
Lemon-Herb Vinegar
Spicy Blueberry Butter
Zucchini Bread-and-Butter Pickles
"Sun-dried" Tomatoes and Roasted Peppers in Garlic-Basil Oil
"Sun-dried" Cherries
Hot-and-Sweet Pepper Relish
Lusty Eggplant Relish

When summer begins to wander away and winter's just around the corner, humans are no different from squirrels—we all like to store things away to be ready for the months ahead. So with the last of the fruits, vegetables, and herbs from the garden, farm stand, or green market, we create treats to enjoy and share and to help bring back memories of that last perfect tomato ripening on the windowsill or a sunny garden full of zucchini.

Berry Vinegar

Makes 3 pints

1 pint very ripe raspberries, strawberries, or blueberries, crushed slightly
1½ quarts white wine vinegar

1. Place the fruit in a sterilized 2-quart jar with a tight-fitting lid and pour the vinegar over it. Close the lid tightly, shake well, and place the jar in a cool, dark place for 3 weeks. Shake the jar daily.

2. Strain the contents of the jar through a colander lined with cheesecloth to remove the fruit. Pour the vinegar into sterilized 1-pint bottles, seal, and store in a cool, dark place.

Lemon-Herb Vinegar

Makes 4 pints

Flavored vinegars, though certainly not a new idea, are still among the most welcome gifts (and incidentally among the easiest to make). Use fresh herbs such as rosemary, oregano, marjoram, thyme, parsley, and basil, alone or in combinations. Or combine them with strong-flavored vegetables such as garlic, hot peppers, or shallots.

2 quarts white wine vinegar *or* red wine vinegar
Peel of 2 lemons, cut into thin strips
4 large sprigs fresh herbs
4 large garlic cloves *or* shallots (optional)
4 small hot red or green peppers (optional)

1. Pour the vinegar into a nonreactive saucepan over medium heat. Heat to the simmering point and remove the pan from the heat.

2. Divide the lemon peel, herbs, and/or garlic, shallots, or hot peppers among 4 pint bottles that have tight-fitting caps or corks. Fit the necks with a funnel, ladle the warm vinegar into the bottles, and cap tightly. Place the bottles in a cool, dark place to age for at least a month before using.

A Few Notes on Canning

- Inspect all produce carefully. Fruits and vegetables should be at their peak, not beyond it. If any signs of bruising or spoilage exist, cut them away completely.
- Always wash canning jars and lids well and sterilize them by boiling for 15 minutes just before using.
- Follow the jar manufacturer's sealing instructions to the letter using clean new lids.
- To be absolutely certain that no spoilage will occur after canning, process all pickles and relishes in a hot-water bath. To do this, place sealed jars at least 1 inch apart on a rack in a large kettle. Pour warm water into the kettle to cover the jars by 2 inches and gradually bring the water to a boil. Boil half-pint jars for 10 minutes, pint jars for 15 minutes, and quart jars for 20 minutes. Remove the jars with tongs and allow to cool gradually before labeling and storing.
- When opening any home-canned jar, if there is any reason at all to think that spoilage has occurred, discard the contents.

Spicy Blueberry Butter

Makes 4 pints

Here's an unusual alternative to other fruit butters. Unorthodox as it seems, it's delicious spread over a thin layer of cream cheese on a hot, toasted bagel.

3 pints blueberries, picked over and washed
4 cups coarsely chopped peeled and cored apples
4 cups sugar
½ teaspoon ground cinnamon
⅛ teaspoon ground mace
⅛ teaspoon ground allspice
⅛ teaspoon grated nutmeg

1. Combine all the ingredients in a medium, heavy saucepan and place over low heat. Cook, stirring frequently, until the sugar dissolves. Turn the heat up to medium-high and, continuing to stir, bring the mixture to a simmer. Return the heat to low and continue simmering, stirring occasionally to prevent sticking, until the mixture is thick, 45 to 50 minutes.

2. Transfer the mixture to sterilized jars and seal. Or allow to cool and pour into jars or plastic containers, cover tightly, and refrigerate.

Zucchini Bread-and-Butter Pickles

Makes 4 quarts

- 1 quart white vinegar
- 1 cup sugar
- ¼ cup salt
- 1 tablespoon celery seeds
- 1 tablespoon dill seeds
- 2 teaspoons mustard seeds
- 8 pounds (4 quarts) small zucchini, cut into ⅛-inch slices
- 5 medium onions, peeled, thinly sliced, and separated into rings

1. Put the vinegar, sugar, salt, and seeds in a large, heavy pot over high heat and bring to a boil. Add the zucchini and onions and cover. Remove from the heat and let stand 1 hour.

2. Return the pot to the stove over high heat. Bring the mixture to a boil again, reduce the heat, and simmer for 3 minutes. Pack the pickles loosely in four sterilized 1-quart jars (or eight 1-pint jars), pour the pickling liquid over to cover, and seal.

3. Process the jars in a boiling-water bath (see page 50) for 20 minutes (15 minutes for 1-pint jars). Cool and label the jars and store in a cool place.

"A gift is as a precious stone in the eyes of him that hath it."
PROVERBS 17:8

"Sun-dried" Tomatoes and Roasted Peppers in Garlic-Basil Oil

This vibrantly colored and flavored combination can be made in any quantity. It's great to have on hand for adding to sandwiches, homemade pizzas, salads, frittatas, and omelets, or for serving as a condiment with thinly sliced flank steak or grilled tuna, bluefish, or swordfish. It also makes a beautiful gift.

Tomatoes can be "sun-dried" by placing them on a rack-lined pan under the hot sun for about 2 days, but the oven-drying method below is a lot easier.

Large ripe red tomatoes
Red or green bell peppers
Peeled whole garlic cloves
Fruity extra-virgin olive oil
Basil leaves

1. Wash and dry the tomatoes and cut them into eighths lengthwise. Using a small spoon, scoop out the seeds and juice. Place a wire rack on a baking sheet and arrange the tomatoes on the rack, skin side up. Allow the tomatoes to drain excess juice for about 1 hour.

2. Set the oven on the warm setting (the temperature should be about 150°F.). Transfer the rack to a clean baking sheet and place in the oven. Dry the tomatoes, turning them every few hours with a spatula, until they are leathery, about 12 hours. Remove them from the oven and allow them to cool on the rack.

3. To roast the peppers, first preheat the broiler and then cut the peppers into halves lengthwise and seed them. Place the peppers skin side up on a baking sheet and broil them, placing them as close as possible to the heat, until the skin chars.

4. Immediately transfer the peppers to a brown paper bag and close the bag, trapping the steam. When the peppers are cool, about 5 minutes, rub off the skins and cut the peppers into ½-inch-wide strips.

"It is said that gifts persuade even the gods."
EURIPIDES

5. Have ready sterilized pint jars and the garlic and basil. Arrange a single layer of tomato strips in the bottom of each jar, followed by a layer of pepper strips. Add a garlic clove and a few basil leaves, keeping the garlic and basil against the side of the jar so they show. Continue layering until all the jars are almost filled but not tightly packed.

6. Carefully pour oil into the jars until about half filled. Tilt the jars and tap them so the oil seeps down, filling any air bubbles and covering the vegetables completely. Add more oil, covering the vegetables and leaving a ⅛-inch space at the top of the jars, and seal. Store in a cool, dark place for at least a week before using and no longer than 3 months.

"Gifts which the giver makes precious are always the most acceptable."
OVID

Packaging Home-Canned Goods for Gifts

Use the prettiest jars or bottles you can find, either saved from store-bought goods or bought at hardware stores or kitchenware shops; old collectible product jars, found at flea markets or antiques shops, work well, too. Cover jar lids with pinked circles or squares of fabric tied on with ribbon or twine, with tags attached that offer serving suggestions.

"Sun-dried" Cherries

Pitted and halved sweet cherries, "sun-dried" by using the method described in steps 1 and 2 of the preceding recipe, make a great snack as is. But they're even better macerated in liqueur to make a luxurious topping for plain chocolate cake and vanilla ice cream. Loosely pack the dried cherries into small jars and pour Kirsch or Amaretto liqueur over the fruit to cover. Cover tightly and let stand for 2 or 3 weeks before using.

Hot-and-Sweet Pepper Relish

Makes approximately 6 half-pints

Simple to make, this colorful, complexly flavored relish is delicious with thin slivers of country ham or grilled smoked pork chops. It also makes a great "instant" hors d'oeuvre. Spread fingers of toasted and cooled pumpernickel bread with a thin layer of cream cheese and add a dab of relish.

- 6 large red bell peppers, seeded and chopped
- 6 large yellow or green bell peppers, seeded and chopped
- 2 jalapeño *or* 3 serrano chili peppers, seeded and chopped
- 4 medium onions, chopped
- 3 cups boiling water, approximately
- 1 cup cider vinegar
- 1¼ cups sugar
- 4 teaspoons salt
- 2 teaspoons celery seed
- 2 teaspoons mustard seed

1. Place the chopped peppers and onions in a large, heavy saucepan with boiling water to cover. Let stand 5 minutes and drain well.

2. While the peppers are draining, place the remaining ingredients in the saucepan. Place over medium-high heat, bring to a boil, and cook 5 minutes. Return the drained peppers and onions to the pan, reduce the heat, and simmer about 10 minutes, or until the vegetables are tender but not mushy.

3. Transfer the relish to sterilized half-pint jars and seal. Process in a boiling-water bath (see page 50) for 15 minutes. Cool, and store in a cool, dry place. Allow to mellow for at least 3 weeks before using, and refrigerate after opening.

Lusty Eggplant Relish

Makes approximately 6 half-pints

Vibrantly colored and flavored, this is an ideal addition to an antipasto tray. It's also the perfect condiment for tucking into a picnic basket and using on sandwiches of country ham, sausages, and/or cheeses on crusty bread.

- 3 pounds small eggplants
- 2 tablespoons salt
- ⅓ cup extra-virgin olive oil
- 1 small onion, thinly sliced and separated into rings
- 1 small red bell pepper, seeded and julienned
- 6 garlic cloves, thinly sliced lengthwise
- 1 tablespoon oregano leaves *or* 1 teaspoon dried oregano
- 1 tablespoon drained capers
- ½ teaspoon dried hot red pepper flakes
- 3 cups white wine vinegar
- 2 tablespoons sugar

1. Peel the eggplant and cut into ⅛-inch julienne strips about 2 inches long. Place the eggplant in a colander, add the salt, and toss well. Cover the colander, place over a large bowl, and let stand 1 hour.

2. Combine the oil, onion, pepper, and garlic in a large, heavy nonreactive Dutch oven or deep skillet, place over medium heat, and sauté the mixture for 5 minutes. Add the eggplant and sauté until golden on all sides, about 5 minutes. Stir in the oregano, capers, and hot pepper flakes.

3. Remove the pan from the heat and divide the eggplant mixture among 6 sterilized half-pint jars. Reserve.

4. Return the Dutch oven to the stove and add the vinegar and sugar. Turn the heat up to high and bring the mixture to a boil. Reduce the heat and simmer for 5 minutes. Remove the pan from the heat and spoon the liquid mixture equally into the 6 eggplant jars, leaving a ¼-inch head space in each jar.

5. Seal the jars and process in a boiling-water bath for 15 minutes (see page 50). Let cool and store in a cool, dark place for 2 to 3 weeks before using.

The Everlasting Garden

Wreaths and Dried Bouquets

Dried Flower Wreaths
Pinecone Wreath
Dried Bouquets

Come late summer and early fall, my house starts to look like an upside-down floral shop, with flowers and herbs hanging just about everywhere to dry. Rather than limiting myself to home-grown varieties, I buy some at the nursery, florist's, or farm stand, and I beg some from the gardens of my friends. Then comes the fun of making big dried bouquets and a variety of wreaths.

"One gift well given recovers many losses."
THOMAS FULLER

Wreath Making—The Basics

According to the myths and legends, the Romans (or was it the Greeks, or maybe the Celts?) were the originators of the wreath. In any case, just about every culture has a tale to tell about wreaths. It seems that most everyone agrees that being round and endless, wreaths symbolize eternity or some sort of lasting good wishes. That's good enough for me.

Here are a few hints for making wreaths. I don't follow a strict method myself: I've made quite a few wreaths over the years and no two have ever been quite alike. For a floral or herb wreath, the point is to gather a wide variety of dried flora with an eye to varying color, scale, and texture—if the combination looks good bunched together beforehand, it will look wonderful as a wreath. A wreath of just two or three things, such as a combination of hydrangea, eucalyptus, and poppy pods, will look wonderful too.

BASIC WREATH-MAKING SUPPLIES

- A base wreath of grapevines, twigs, straw, or Styrofoam
- Florist wire (available at floral supply shops)
- Florist picks (available at floral supply shops)
- Glue (Elmer's, Sobo, or a hot-glue gun)

WREATH-MAKING INGREDIENTS

Dried flowers: statice, baby's breath, roses and rosebuds, asters, strawflowers, miniature mums, heather, coxcomb, lavender, hydrangea, marigolds, zinnias, delphiniums, alfalfa, thistles, milkweed, goldenrod

Dried herbs: rosemary, bay leaves, sage, chive blossoms, mint, marjoram, thyme, yarrow

Miscellaneous: eucalyptus, poppy pods, wheat, oats, pinecones, bayberry, bittersweet, winterberry, pussy willows in spring, dried peppers, nuts, cinnamon sticks, small ears of Indian corn, branches of fall leaves

Dried Flower Wreath

1. Start with a grapevine wreath for the underbase (here it's heart-shaped; for the wreath on page 63, a round one was used) and dried flowers selected for a variety of color and texture.

2. Glue on a neutral base layer (here it's sparsely placed eucalyptus; for the wreath on page 63, a full base of baby's breath was used). The wreath is finished with more flowers and a twining ribbon.

Pinecone Wreath

1. The first step in making a pinecone and nut wreath is wiring groups of two or three pinecones together and then wiring each bunch onto a floral pick.

2. The pinecone bunches are stuck into the base wreath of straw or Styrofoam, tightly covering the face and sides so the base doesn't show through.

3. Finish the wreath by gluing a variety of unshelled nuts (walnuts, hazelnuts, brazil nuts, pecans, etc.) between and around the pinecones.

An elaborate bouquet of dried flowers, with thistles, eucalyptus, and wheat.

A simple bouquet of ribbon-tied roses and lavender can be hung anywhere.

Heather, red berries, tiny white wildflowers, and strips of moss were added to a bought wreath of huckleberry vines.

Drying Flowers and Herbs

This is really a simple task. Tie small bunches of flowers or herbs together with kitchen string (larger flowers can be tied into proportionally larger bunches) and hang in a well-ventilated, dry, but not too hot place. I hang them from an old wooden clothes-drying rack as well as from extra hooks just about anywhere in the house that's not too sunny.

Small, delicate flowers such as roses can be dried with little loss of color by placing them in a shallow bed of silica gel (available at floral supply shops). Cover the flowers with the gel, and let them stand for a week. Remove the dried flowers from the gel very carefully.

This wreath was made several years ago and is periodically rejuvenated with the addition of more bright-colored flowers.

From the Autumn Orchard

Apples, Pears, Figs, and Quince

I grew up in Johnny Appleseed country, and in addition to the apple, pear, crab-apple, and other fruit trees we had in our small orchard, there were wild apple trees in the woods beyond the farm. So we always had plenty of apples around, and Mom was always baking pies and putting up jars and jars of applesauce. Apple pies and sauce are still among my favorite foods, but I like experimenting with other recipes and other fruits, too.

Golden Harvest Chutney

Makes about 8 half-pints

Here's a zesty combination of pears, apples, and the last of the not-quite-ripe tomatoes from the garden—perfect with roasted pork, ham, or chicken.

- 2 cups peeled, cored, and diced firm ripe pears
- 3 cups peeled, cored, and diced tart apples
- 3 cups peeled, seeded, and diced not-quite-ripe tomatoes
- 1 cup golden raisins
- 1½ cups halved seedless (or seeded) green grapes
- Grated rind of 1 lemon
- 2 medium onions, chopped
- 1 large garlic clove, finely chopped
- 1 yellow or red bell pepper, seeded and diced
- 1¼ cups light brown sugar
- 1 cup white vinegar
- 1 teaspoon dry mustard
- 1 teaspoon ground ginger
- ¼ teaspoon cayenne pepper

1. In a large, heavy, nonreactive saucepan, combine all the ingredients and cover the pan. Place over low heat and bring to a simmer, stirring occasionally. Continue cooking until the fruits are quite tender and the liquid is very thick and syrupy, 50 minutes to an hour.

2. Transfer the mixture to sterilized half-pint jars and seal. Process in a boiling-water bath (page 50) for 10 minutes, cool, and store in a cool, dark place.

Spiced Sugar Pears

Makes 4 to 5 pints

We had a sugar pear tree in our orchard on the farm and always looked forward to the fruit. (Sugar pears are more widely known as seckel pears.) Here's how Mom used to put them up. They make a rather elegant dessert warmed and served with a dollop of good butter almond ice cream and a sprinkling of lightly toasted sliced almonds.

3 cups cider vinegar
2 cups water
2 cups light brown sugar
2 cups granulated sugar
3 cinnamon sticks
2 tablespoons whole cloves
1 tablespoon whole allspice
1 1-inch piece vanilla bean
5 pounds firm-ripe sugar (seckel) pears

1. In a large kettle or stockpot, combine the vinegar, water, sugars, spices, and vanilla bean. Place over medium-high heat and bring to a boil, stirring until the sugar is dissolved. Reduce the heat to low and let the mixture simmer.

2. Peel the pears, leaving the stems on. Immediately place the pears in the simmering syrup. Cover the kettle and simmer the pears until just tender, about 15 minutes. Remove the vanilla bean.

3. Transfer the pears to sterilized pint or quart jars and cover with syrup, leaving a ¼-inch head space in each jar. Seal the jars and process for 15 minutes (20 minutes for quarts) in a boiling-water bath (page 50). Let cool and store in a cool, dark place.

Spicy-Hot Sugar Pears For a savory variation delicious with ham, roast pork, or roast or grilled duck, omit the vanilla bean and add a whole peeled garlic clove and ¼ teaspoon cayenne pepper at the end of step 1. Remove the garlic at the end of step 2.

Rosy Quince Marmalade

Makes about 8 half-pints

A touch of ginger and cinnamon adds a hint of piquancy to this pretty jelly. Choose pale yellow, ripe, but unbruised quinces.

6 cups water
6 cups sugar
4 pounds quinces
Juice and grated rind of 4 lemons
2 tablespoons grated gingerroot
1 small cinnamon stick

1. Combine the water and sugar in a large, heavy, nonreactive saucepan. Place over medium-high heat and bring to a boil. Boil 3 minutes and then reduce the heat to low.

2. Peel and core the quinces and then grate them coarsely. Add the quinces and the remaining ingredients to the pan and simmer until the quince is tender, about 30 minutes. Turn up the heat and boil the mixture until the liquid is very thick and syrupy and sheets when dropped from the side of a spoon (220°F. on a candy thermometer).

3. Transfer the mixture to sterilized half-pint jars, seal, and process in a boiling-water bath (page 50) for 10 minutes. Cool and store in a cool place.

Rummy Fig Preserves

Makes about 8 half-pints

Fig season starts in the summer and runs into fall, but they always seem more fall-like to me. Aside from the usual uses, try these rich preserves warm over ice cream with a sprinkling of toasted nuts.

6 cups sugar
4 pounds figs, peeled and coarsely chopped
Juice and grated rind of 1 lemon
1 cup dark rum

1. Combine all the ingredients in a large, heavy, nonreactive saucepan and cover it. Place over low heat and cook, stirring occasionally to prevent sticking, until all the sugar is dissolved, 40 to 45 minutes.

2. Uncover the pan and raise the heat to medium low. Continue cooking, stirring occasionally, until the figs are translucent and the mixture is thick and syrupy, about 45 to 50 minutes longer. Remove from the heat and let the mixture stand overnight.

3. Bring the mixture to a simmer again over low heat and simmer for 5 minutes. Pack the mixture into sterilized jars and seal. Process in a boiling-water bath (page 50) for 10 minutes. Cool and store in a cool, dark place.

CRABAPPLE-SAGE JELLY

Makes about 6 half-pints

Delicious with the Thanksgiving bird, as well as roasted pork, duck, or chicken.

3 pounds crabapples
3 large garlic cloves, crushed
1 cup white wine vinegar
Juice of 3 lemons
4 cups sugar, approximately (see step 3)
1 cup loosely packed sage leaves, plus 6 small sprigs

1. Coarsely chop the apples; do not peel and core them. In a large, heavy, nonreactive saucepan, combine the apples, garlic, vinegar, and lemon juice. Add water to just cover the apples and place the pan over medium heat. Bring the mixture to a simmer and cook until apples are very soft and mushy, 20 to 25 minutes.

2. Remove the pan from the heat and allow it to stand for 10 minutes to cool slightly. Strain the mixture through a sieve lined with a double thickness of cheesecloth. Let the last of the mixture drip through the cloth rather than pressing the fruit through.

3. Measure the liquid and stir in an equal amount of sugar (1 cup sugar for every cup of liquid). Return the mixture to the pan and clip a candy thermometer onto the rim. Place over medium-high heat and bring the mixture to a boil. Cook, stirring occasionally, until the mixture reaches the sheeting stage (220°F. on a candy thermometer), about 30 minutes.

4. Stir in 1 cup sage leaves and turn off the heat. Cover the pan and allow to stand for 20 minutes. Strain the mixture again to remove the herbs.

5. Place a sage sprig in each of 6 sterilized half-pint jars. Transfer the jelly to the sterilized jars and seal. Cool and label the jars and store in a cool, dark place.

VARIATIONS Substitute rosemary or basil for the sage. With any of the herbs, add a crushed whole clove of garlic in step 1 and remove it in step 2.

October Cake

Makes one 10-inch tube cake

This fragrant and moist cake travels and keeps well—in fact, it's best a day or two after it's baked. Top each slice with a big dollop of unsweetened whipped cream.

1 cup chopped dates
3 cups sifted cake flour
1 tablespoon baking powder
½ teaspoon salt
1 teaspoon ground cinnamon
1 teaspoon ground ginger
½ teaspoon grated nutmeg
¾ cup vegetable shortening
1½ cups firmly packed dark brown sugar
3 large eggs
1 tablespoon lemon juice
1 cup fresh apple cider
1½ cups chopped firm apples or pears, or half of each
1 cup chopped walnuts or pecans
Confectioners' sugar, for dusting

1. Preheat the oven to 350°F. Grease a 10-inch tube pan. In a small bowl, toss the dates with 2 or 3 tablespoons of the flour to prevent them from sticking together. Reserve.

2. In a large mixing bowl, sift together the remaining flour, baking powder, salt, and spices. In a separate bowl, cream the shortening and brown sugar until light and fluffy, then beat in the eggs one at a time.

3. A third at a time, alternately beat the wet mixture and the cider into the dry ingredients until the batter is completely blended and smooth. Fold the apples, dates, and nuts into the batter and transfer the batter to the prepared pan.

4. Bake until the cake is well browned and a cake tester comes out clean, 50 to 55 minutes. Invert the cake onto a wire rack to cool completely and then dust with confectioners' sugar.

◆ The cake can be packed in a large, round decorative tin or wrapped in cellophane and tied with ribbon; tuck a few colorful fall leaves into the bow.

Apple-Cheddar Bread

Makes two 8½ × 4½-inch loaves

This hearty bread has a complex flavor thanks to the combination of whole-wheat flour, Cheddar, and toasted walnuts. Serve it plain or toasted with only a thin spreading of cream cheese or cottage cheese, and applesauce.

- 1½ cups all-purpose flour
- 1½ cups whole-wheat flour
- ½ teaspoon salt
- ¼ teaspoon ground cinnamon
- 1 tablespoon baking powder
- ¼ cup vegetable shortening
- ½ cup sugar
- 1 large egg
- 1¾ cups milk
- 1½ cups chopped tart apples
- 1 cup coarsely grated sharp Cheddar
- 1 cup chopped toasted walnuts (see page 71)

1. Preheat the oven to 350°F. Grease two 8½ × 4½-inch loaf pans.

2. Into a large mixing bowl, sift together the flours, salt, cinnamon, and baking powder. In a separate bowl, cream the shortening and sugar together and then beat in the egg and milk.

3. Pour the liquid mixture over the dry mixture and beat with a large spoon just until all the dry ingredients are moistened. Stir in the apples, cheese, and nuts. Divide the batter between the two prepared pans.

4. Bake the bread until the top is well browned and a cake tester inserted in the center of a loaf comes out clean, 50 to 60 minutes. Transfer the pans to a wire rack and cool 10 minutes. Remove the loaves from the pans and place them, on their sides, on the rack to cool completely. Wrap the loaves tightly in plastic wrap and store in the refrigerator up to three days.

◆ The plastic-wrapped loaves can be wrapped and tied like any boxed gift, or rewrap the loaves in clear cellophane and tie them up in wide, colorful ribbon.

Trick-Or-Treats

FOR CHILDREN OF ALL AGES

Crazy Chip Cookies
Pecan-Cashew Popcorn Balls
Nutty Cinnamon Bowties
Hazelnut Candy Apples

Mom loves telling stories of long-ago Halloweens and the mischief she and her cronies caused back when they were kids, on those spooky country nights when trick-or-treating meant more tricking than treating. Here are a few of my favorite pranks, "innocent" as they were, that she and her pals used to pull: soaping car windows, knocking down the gathered corn shocks in a farmer's field, tossing pebbles or corn kernels at a neighbor's front door, or even tipping over an outhouse and then "running like the devil!" So much for the tricks; here a few treats.

A basket of squashes, gourds, fall leaves, and bittersweet.

Toasting Nuts

When nuts are included in cookies or cakes, we want them for their flavor as well as their crunch, and the flavor of just about any nut can benefit from a light toasting. To toast nuts, spread them in an even single layer on a baking sheet and place them in a 350°F. oven until they brown slightly, about 10 minutes. Cool the nuts before using them in cookies or cakes.

CRAZY CHIP COOKIES

Makes about 7 dozen

No one can ever guess what gives these cookies their light, crunchy texture, but when kids find out it's potato chips, they're always fascinated. My nephew Larry sent me this recipe, which he in turn got from his Grandma Huffman.

- 2 cups (4 sticks) butter, softened
- 1 cup sugar
- 1 teaspoon vanilla extract
- 3½ cups flour
- 1½ cups crushed potato chips
- 1 cup chopped walnuts
- 1½ cups M&M–type candies
- Flour for rolling

1. Preheat the oven to 350°F. In a mixing bowl, cream together the butter, sugar, and vanilla until light and fluffy. Beat in the flour, then add the potato chips, nuts, and 1 cup candies and mix well.

2. Roll the dough into ¾-inch balls and roll each ball lightly in flour. Place the balls onto *ungreased* cookie sheets about 2 inches apart. Lightly press with a fork to flatten slightly and press a few of the remaining candies into each cookie.

3. Bake until the cookies are golden brown, 10 to 12 minutes, and remove to wire racks to cool. Store in tightly covered tins in a cool place.

"Once in a young lifetime one should be allowed to have as much sweetness as one can possibly want and hold."

JUDITH OLNEY

PECAN-CASHEW POPCORN BALLS

Makes 2 dozen 3-inch balls

- 1 cup granulated sugar
- 1 cup firmly packed light brown sugar
- 1 cup light corn syrup
- ⅔ cup water
- 1 pound (4 sticks) butter
- 2 cups pecan halves, lightly toasted (see page 71)
- 2 cups roasted cashews, lightly toasted
- 8 cups freshly popped popcorn

1. Combine the sugars, corn syrup, and water in a heavy pan fitted with a candy thermometer and place over high heat. Bring the mixture to a boil and add the butter, stirring until it has melted. Continue cooking until the mixture reaches 350°F., 20 to 30 minutes.

2. In a large, lightly oiled bowl, toss the nuts and popcorn together. Carefully pour the hot syrup over the popcorn-nut mixture. Carefully but quickly toss the mixture with a long-handled wooden spoon to coat the popcorn and nuts completely with syrup.

3. As soon as the mixture is cool enough to handle, quickly shape into 3-inch balls and place the balls on a nonstick or lightly oiled baking sheet to cool. Store, tightly wrapped, in a cool place.

◆ Wrap popcorn balls individually in squares of amber cellophane, tied up with gold or orange and black ribbons. Or pile the balls together into a basket with red apples and wrap the basket in cellophane with orange and black ribbon. Or place the balls in a brown paper bag and tie with ribbon.

NUTTY CINNAMON BOWTIES

Makes about 7 dozen

- 1 cup (2 sticks) butter, softened
- 1 8-ounce package cream cheese, softened
- 2½ cups all-purpose flour
- 1 cup sugar
- 2 teaspoons ground cinnamon
- ⅔ cup finely chopped pecans or walnuts
- 1 large egg, well beaten

1. In a large mixing bowl, beat together the butter and cream cheese until well blended and then gradually beat in the flour. Form the dough into a ball and chill for 3 hours or so.

2. In a small bowl, stir together the sugar and cinnamon and then stir in the nuts. Set aside.

3. Preheat the oven to 400°F. Remove the dough from the refrigerator and roll it into a rectangle about ¼-inch thick.

Brush the surface of the dough with the beaten egg and then scatter the nut mixture evenly over all and lightly press it into the dough.

4. Cut the dough into strips about ½″ × 3″. Twist each strip 360 degrees to form a bowtie shape and place them on the cookie sheets. Bake until golden brown, 10 to 12 minutes. Cool the cookies on wire racks and store in tightly covered tins in a cool place.

Hazelnut Candy Apples

Makes 12 apples

- 3¼ cups sugar
- ⅔ cups butter
- 3 tablespoons cider vinegar
- 3 tablespoons boiling water
- 1½ cups finely chopped lightly toasted hazelnuts (see page 71)
- 8 medium "eating" apples, such as McIntosh, Macoun, Greening, or Jonathan, washed and well dried

1. In a small, heavy saucepan over low heat, combine the sugar, butter, vinegar, and boiling water. Cook, stirring constantly, until the sugar is dissolved, then turn up the heat and bring to a boil. Continue cooking (do not stir) until the mixture reaches the hard ball stage, 250°F. on a candy thermometer (see Note).

2. While the syrup is cooking, spread an 18-inch piece of wax paper out on the work surface. Place the nuts in a wide, shallow bowl. Skewer the apples with wooden popsicle sticks or candy-apple sticks.

3. When the syrup is ready, remove it from the heat. Working quickly, dip the apples, one at a time, into the syrup, rolling them to coat them completely (the last few may need the help of a spoon). Immediately dip each coated apple into the nuts to coat the bottom third of the apple. Place the apples onto the wax paper to allow them to harden and cool.

4. Cut 10-inch squares of wax paper or cellophane. One at a time, stand a cooled apple in the center of a square and pull up the corners and twist them around the stick. Tie each apple with a colorful ribbon or brown twine. Store the apples in the refrigerator or another cool place.

NOTE Lacking a candy thermometer, the hard ball stage can be tested by dropping a teaspoonful of syrup into cold water. When the syrup forms a ball that is quite firm but still pliable, the hard ball stage has been reached.

REETINGS

CHRISTMAS

Cookies for Santa and Other Friends

A Baker's Half-Dozen or So

Lemon Stars
Jam Thumbprints
Fudge Hermits
Nolan's Icebox Butterscotch Slices
Ginger-Molasses "Slipware" Cookies
Spice Pinwheels
Poppyseed Petticoat Tails
Jamboree Bars

To paraphrase Will Rogers, I've never met a man who didn't like cookies (or a woman or child either, for that matter). And I've never met anyone who doesn't appreciate receiving a package of home-baked cookies at Christmastime. A lot of folks I know bake exactly the same kinds of cookies every year, never wavering. I'm pretty much a traditionalist too, but since Christmas is a season of surprises, I always like to try a few new kinds. Here are some current favorites (and don't forget everyone's favorite, chocolate chip cookies—the best recipe is right on the back of the chocolate chip package!).

Lemon Stars

Makes 4 to 5 dozen cookies, depending on the cutters.

This dough is a great all-purpose one for cutout Christmas cookies; this year I decided to make a variety of stars.

- ¾ cup (1½ sticks) butter, softened
- 1 3-ounce package cream cheese, softened
- ¾ cup sugar
- 2 cups all-purpose flour
- ¼ teaspoon baking soda
- ¼ teaspoon baking powder
- ¼ teaspoon salt
- Juice and grated rind of 1 lemon
- 1 teaspoon vanilla extract
- 1 large egg white
- Granulated sugar or colored sugars, for decorating

1. In the bowl of an electric mixer, cream the butter, cream cheese, and ¾ cup sugar together until light and fluffy. Add the flour, baking soda, baking powder, and salt and beat on low speed until the mixture is smooth. Add the lemon juice and rind and the vanilla and beat until blended.

2. Roll the dough into a ball, wrap in wax paper or plastic wrap, and refrigerate until firm, about 1 hour.

3. Preheat the oven to 350°F. Roll out the dough to a thickness of about ⅛ inch. Using floured star-shaped cutters, cut out the dough and place the cookies about 1 inch apart on *ungreased* cookie sheets.

4. Brush the surface with the egg white, sprinkle liberally with sugar, and bake until the edges are golden, about 10 minutes. Remove to wire racks to cool and store in tightly covered tin containers in a cool place.

Jam Thumbprints Christmas just wouldn't be Christmas without these. Omit the lemon juice and rind. Transfer the soft dough to a pastry tube fitted with a large star tip and pipe 1½-inch rosettes about 2 inches apart onto ungreased baking sheets. Using a floured fingertip, make a depression in the center of each rosette and spoon ¼ teaspoonful of seedless raspberry jam into each. Bake until very lightly browned, 8 to 10 minutes.

Fudge Hermits

Makes about 4 dozen cookies

These spicy and chocolaty cookies tend to disappear quickly, so you may want to double the recipe.

½ cup firmly packed brown sugar
½ cup granulated sugar
½ cup vegetable shortening
1 large egg, lightly beaten
3 ounces unsweetened chocolate, melted and cooled
⅓ cup milk
1½ teaspoons vanilla extract
1⅓ cups sifted all-purpose flour
2 teaspoons baking powder
¼ teaspoon salt
2 teaspoons ground cinnamon
¾ teaspoon ground ginger
1½ cups raisins
1 cup chopped walnuts

1. Preheat the oven to 350°F. Grease baking sheets.

2. In a large mixing bowl, cream together the sugars and shortening until light and fluffy. Beat in the egg, then the cooled chocolate, milk, and vanilla. Into a separate bowl, sift together the flour, baking powder, salt, and spices. Add the dry mixture to the wet mixture and beat until smooth, then stir in the raisins and nuts.

3. Drop the dough by teaspoonfuls onto the prepared sheets, about 2 inches apart. Bake until the edges are browned, about 15 minutes. Remove to wire racks to cool. Pack the cookies in wax paper–lined tins and tuck a slice of apple into the tins to keep the cookies moist and chewy.

ICED FUDGE HERMITS Drizzle the cooled cookies with the icing on pages 80 to 81 (do not add coloring to the icing).

Nolan's Icebox Butterscotch Slices

Makes about 8 dozen cookies

3½ cups sifted cake flour
2½ teaspoons baking powder
½ teaspoon salt
1 cup (2 sticks) butter
1½ cups firmly packed dark brown sugar
2 large eggs
1½ teaspoons vanilla extract
1½ teaspoons milk
2 cups chopped walnuts

Some of these old tins, filled with Christmas cookies, have passed back and forth in our family for years.

1. Into a mixing bowl, sift together the flour, baking powder, and salt. In a separate bowl, cream the butter and brown sugar together until light and fluffy. Add the eggs, one at a time, beating thoroughly each time. Beat the dry mixture into the wet mixture and then beat in the vanilla, the milk, and 1 cup of the nuts.

2. Divide the dough in half and shape each half into a cylinder about 1½ inches in diameter. Roll the cylinders in the remaining nuts to coat them evenly. Wrap the dough in wax paper or plastic wrap and refrigerate for 4 hours or overnight.

3. Preheat the oven to 425°F. Lightly grease baking sheets.

4. Unwrap the dough cylinders and cut into ⅛-inch-thick slices. Place the slices about 1 inch apart on the baking sheets. Bake until golden brown, 5 to 6 minutes. Remove to wire racks to cool, and store in tightly covered tins.

Packing Up Cookies for Giving

- If you're taking your gift of cookies to its destination yourself, arrange them on a pretty glass plate or platter and wrap in red or amber cellophane tied with a gold ribbon.
- When packing delicate cookies for shipping, arrange them in a pretty wax paper–lined tin in single layers, with a thin layer of popcorn between each layer. Wrap the tin in bubble pack and then pack snugly into a cardboard box.
- Tuck a small tin or box of cookies into the box with another gift as a little extra surprise. Or pack a small package of cookies into a basket with a few other homemade edibles.

Ginger-Molasses "Slipware" Cookies

Makes 3 to 4 dozen,
depending on the size of the cutters

Both the familiar flavor of these holiday cookies (like old-fashioned gingerbread) and their appearance (cut and decorated to look like red-brown slipware) are more than a century old.

½ cup (1 stick) butter, melted and cooled
½ cup vegetable shortening, melted and cooled
1 cup light molasses
2 large eggs
Grated rind of 1 lemon
4½ cups sifted all-purpose flour
1 teaspoon baking soda
1 teaspoon salt
4 teaspoons ground ginger
1 teaspoon ground cinnamon

ICING
1 to 1½ cups confectioners' sugar
1 large egg white
Yellow food coloring

1. In a mixing bowl, combine the butter, shortening, molasses, 1 egg, and the lemon rind and beat until well blended. Into a separate bowl, sift together the flour, baking soda, salt, and spices. Gradually beat the dry mixture into the wet mixture until well blended. Form the dough into a ball, wrap in wax paper or plastic wrap, and refrigerate until firm, 4 hours or overnight.

2. Preheat the oven to 375°F. Lightly grease cookie sheets.

3. Divide the dough ball in two and roll each half to a scant ⅛-inch thickness. Cut out the dough using cookie cutters (I use simple shapes such as hearts, bells, stars, and circles with fluted edges). Place the cookies about 1 inch apart on the greased baking sheets.

4. Beat the remaining egg with 1 tablespoon water and brush the surface of the dough lightly with the egg glaze. Bake the cookies until the edges are browned, 12 to 15 minutes. Cool the cookies for 5 minutes on the baking sheets and then transfer to wire racks to cool completely.

5. To make the icing, beat together 1

cup confectioners' sugar and the egg white to make a smooth icing just thin enough to squeeze through a pastry tube; beat in more confectioners' sugar, if necessary. Add a drop or two of food coloring to tint the icing a golden yellow.

6. Spoon the icing into a pastry tube fitted with a small, plain "writing" tip (number 3) and pipe designs, names, and holiday greetings onto the cookies. Allow the icing to harden completely before packing the cookies, with wax paper between each layer, into tightly covered containers.

Spice Pinwheels

Makes about 7 dozen

Cardamom adds an unexpected old-fashioned flavor to these pretty cookies, which are especially good with a cup of hot tea. Plan to make the dough a day before baking.

1 cup (2 sticks) butter, softened
2 cups sugar
2 large eggs, lightly beaten
2 teaspoons vanilla extract
1 teaspoon grated lemon rind
3 cups sifted all-purpose flour
½ teaspoon salt
1 tablespoon baking powder
2 teaspoons ground cardamom
1 teaspoon ground cinnamon
½ teaspoon ground cloves
½ teaspoon grated nutmeg

1. In a mixing bowl, beat the butter until light and fluffy, then gradually beat in the sugar. Beat in the eggs one at a time, then the vanilla and lemon rind. Into a separate bowl, sift together the flour, salt, and baking powder. Gradually beat the dry ingredients into the wet mixture, forming a soft dough.

2. Divide the dough in half. Return one half to the mixing bowl and beat in the spices. Divide each dough half in two, wrap, and chill until firm but pliable, 1 or 2 hours.

3. Roll each piece into equally sized rectangles, ⅛ inch thick. Place a spice rectangle on top of a plain one and roll into long cylinders. Wrap the two cylinders and chill until quite firm, 8 hours or overnight.

4. Preheat the oven to 400°F. Lightly grease baking sheets.

5. One cylinder at a time, cut off ⅛-inch slices and place on the baking sheets. Bake until the edges are golden brown, 8 to 10 minutes, and remove to wire racks to cool. Store in tightly covered containers in a cool place.

POPPYSEED PETTICOAT TAILS

Makes 2 dozen cookies

There are several stories telling how these thin, crisp, shortbreadlike cookies got their name: It's either a derivation from the French *petites gatelles*, meaning small cakes, or from the fact that the shape of the cookies resembles starchy white petticoats.

1 cup (2 sticks) butter, softened
½ cup confectioners' sugar
⅛ teaspoon salt
1 teaspoon vanilla extract
2 cups all-purpose flour
2 tablespoons poppyseeds
Confectioners' sugar, for dusting

1. Preheat the oven to 300°F. Generously butter two 8-inch round cake pans.

2. In a mixing bowl, cream the butter, ½ cup confectioners' sugar, and salt together until light and fluffy, then beat in the vanilla. Add the flour and knead to form a stiff dough. Add the poppyseeds and knead them into the dough.

3. Divide the dough into two equal parts and press each part into a pan. Prick the dough all over with a fork and then score each circle into 12 wedges. Bake until golden brown (petticoat tails should be slightly browner than traditional shortbread), 35 to 40 minutes.

4. Remove the pans from the oven and cut along the scored lines. Place the pans on wire racks to cool. Remove the cookies from the pans, dust liberally with confectioners' sugar, and store in tightly covered containers in a cool, dry place.

The Christmas Cookie Club

Here's a way to make only one kind of cookie and end up with a vast array, *and* have an easy party as part of the bargain: Make eleven dozen of your favorite cookies and wrap each dozen individually. Call nine friends or family members and ask them to do the same. Invite all the participants over and have them bring all but one dozen of their cookies. Put on a big pot of coffee and put out a dozen of each kind of cookie for everyone to sample. As the guests leave, have them exchange cookies with one another. Everyone goes home with a full stomach and a cookie storehouse!

Jamboree Bars

Makes about 3 dozen cookies

❧

These easy cookies are rich, buttery, crunchy, fruity, nutty, and coconutty. 'Nough said.

- ½ cup (1 stick) butter
- ½ teaspoon salt
- 1½ cups firmly packed dark brown sugar
- 1 cup sifted all-purpose flour
- 2 large eggs
- 1 teaspoon vanilla extract
- 2 tablespoons all-purpose flour
- ½ teaspoon baking powder
- 1½ cups shredded coconut
- 1 cup chopped walnuts or pecans
- ¼ cup smooth raspberry or strawberry jam

1. Preheat the oven to 325°F. In a small mixing bowl, cream together the butter, salt, and ½ cup of the brown sugar, then blend in the sifted flour.

2. Spread the dough evenly in the bottom of a greased 9-inch square cake pan with straight sides. Bake for 15 minutes, or until lightly browned. Remove from the oven to a wire rack and let cool for 5 minutes.

3. Combine the remaining cup of brown sugar, the eggs, and the vanilla and beat until foamy and thick, then beat in the 2 tablespoons flour and the baking powder. Stir in the coconut and the nuts.

4. Spread the jam evenly over the dough in the pan, then carefully spread the coconut-nut mixture over the jam. Return the pan to the oven and bake about 25 minutes, or until the surface is nicely browned. Remove the pan from the oven to a wire rack and allow to cool completely.

5. Cut into 1 × 2-inch bars. Store the cookies in a wax paper–lined container, tightly covered.

❧

"The best Christmas gift one can bestow on a child or a friend is a happy memory."

THE NEW YORK TIMES

December 23, 1894

From Under the Tree

GOOD THINGS FOR THE CHRISTMAS DAY TABLE

Yorkshire Yule Bread
Uncle John's Cranberry-Walnut Ketchup
Old-Fashioned Cranberry Relish
Steamed Figgy Pudding
Orange Rum Butter
Hazelnut-Coconut Brittle
Apricot-Almond Snowballs
My Special Holiday Cordial

Our traditional centerpiece of fruit, pinecones, holly, and candles in a big basket.

When we were children we didn't have much spending money, so we used to make simple little gifts at Christmastime, and it always amazed me that the gifts were always opened up with big smiles. Now, of course, I realize that these presents, no matter how crudely made, were received for what they were: simple expressions of love and caring. So I've continued the tradition into adulthood, and my homemade holiday presents are still always greeted with smiles.

YORKSHIRE YULE BREAD

Makes one 8-inch round loaf

A traditional Christmas bread in England, this is great at breakfast-time. This bread freezes perfectly, so it can easily be made long before the holidays.

3½ to 4 cups all-purpose flour
½ teaspoon ground cinnamon
½ teaspoon ground cloves
½ teaspoon ground ginger
½ teaspoon grated nutmeg
2 packages active dry yeast

¾ cup warm milk
½ cup sugar
⅛ teaspoon salt
1 large egg, lightly beaten
½ cup (1 stick) butter, melted
¼ cup dried currants
¼ cup golden raisins
¼ cup candied orange or lemon peel
Confectioners' sugar, for dusting

1. Into a medium bowl, sift together 1 cup of the flour and the four spices. Reserve.

2. In a large bowl, stir the yeast and warm milk together to dissolve the yeast. Stir in the sugar, salt, and egg. Mix in the flour mixture, then gradually beat in the butter. Add more flour, ½ cup at a time, until a not-too-sticky dough is formed. Mix in the fruit and the peel.

3. Turn out the dough onto a floured work surface. Clean the bowl and oil it lightly. Knead the dough, adding a bit more flour if needed to keep it from being too sticky, until it is satiny and elastic. Form it into a ball, place in the bowl, cover with a cloth, and let rise until doubled in bulk, about 1 hour.

4. Lightly butter a small baking sheet. Punch the dough down and knead it for about 5 minutes. Shape the dough into a ball again, place it on the baking sheet, and cut 3 crisscross slashes ½ inch into the surface, making a star. Cover the dough and let rise again to doubled in bulk, about 45 minutes.

5. Preheat the oven to 375°F. Bake the bread until it is nicely browned and sounds hollow when tapped with a finger, 35 to 40 minutes. Transfer the loaf to a wire rack to cool. Dust the bread lightly with confectioners' sugar before serving.

Uncle John's Cranberry-Walnut Ketchup

Makes about 6 half-pints

This recipe has already appeared a few books ago in *Special Occasions*, but it's my favorite homemade Christmas gift, so I can't help but include it again here. My friends and family, who swear they'll eat this "on anything," have come to expect a jar under the tree every year.

- 2 large onions, coarsely chopped
- 1 large tart apple, peeled, cored, and coarsely chopped
- 1 large garlic clove, finely chopped
- 1 tablespoon finely chopped gingerroot (see Note)
- 1 teaspoon grated orange rind
- 1 cup orange juice
- 6 cups (2 12-ounce bags) cranberries
- 2 cups firmly packed light brown sugar
- 1½ cups finely chopped walnuts, lightly toasted (see page 71)
- 1 cup cider vinegar
- 1 teaspoon ground cinnamon
- 1 teaspoon ground cloves
- ½ teaspoon salt
- ½ teaspoon freshly ground black pepper

1. Put the onions, apple, garlic, ginger, orange rind, and water in a large, heavy saucepan over medium heat, and bring the mixture to a boil. Lower the heat and simmer for 10 minutes. Add the cranberries to the pan, bring to a simmer again, and cook, stirring frequently, until all the cranberries "pop."

2. Puree the mixture in the bowl of a food processor fitted with the steel chopping blade (or use a food mill) and return the puree to the pan. Stir in the remaining ingredients. Place the pan over high heat and bring the mixture to a rolling boil, stirring constantly.

3. Ladle the ketchup into 6 sterilized half-pint jars and seal. Process the jars in a boiling-water bath (page 50) for 10 minutes. Cool and label the jars and store in a cool, dark place.

◆ Cover the jar lids with pinked circles of burgundy and forest green plaid or paisley fabric. Tie with gold or silver

cord, with tiny pinecones or a sprig of holly tied to the bow.

NOTE If fresh gingerroot is absolutely unavailable, substitute 1 teaspoon ground ginger and add it in step 2.

Old-fashioned Cranberry Relish

Makes about 3 half-pints

This tangy relish, the kind that everyone's grandmother used to make, takes only a few minutes. Not just for turkey, it's delicious with ham, pork, and especially roast duck. The relish can be made in the food processor, but I like the texture (not to mention the authenticity) of using an old-fashioned hand food grinder. This relish will keep for weeks and weeks in the refrigerator.

1 medium orange
½ lemon
1 medium tart apple
3 cups (1 12-ounce bag) cranberries
½ cup sugar
¼ teaspoon ground cloves

1. Quarter the orange and lemon and remove the seeds. Quarter the apple and core it. Do not peel the fruit.

2. Grind all the fruit, place in a bowl, and stir in the sugar and cloves. Transfer to half-pint jars, cover, and refrigerate for at least two days before using.

Christmas Scents

Here are a few ideas for giving the "essence" of Christmas.

- Instead of the more usual garlands of popcorn and berries, string together dried apple slices, strips of orange rind, cinnamon sticks, and cranberries on brown twine. When the garlands are hung, the entire house will smell like Christmas.
- Using small scraps of loosely woven fabric, stitch up small sachet pillows filled with fragrant pine needles. The pillows can be square and tied up with ribbons like packages, or shaped like the gingerbread man I received one year. He was made of brown wool, with red buttons for his eyes and nose and white rickrack stitched on to stimulate icing.
- Make a Christmas potpourri (see basic potpourri recipe and packaging suggestions on pages 40 to 41) using tiny whole dried roses, rose petals, pine needles and tiny pinecones, strips of orange rind, bay leaves, cinnamon sticks, whole cloves, and allspice.
- Give a dozen bayberry- or spice-scented candles with a pair of brass candlesticks, either new or old.

Steamed Figgy Pudding

Serves 6 to 8

Here's an old-fashioned and almost forgotten Christmastime dessert that's perfectly giftable in a new or antique pudding mold. The recipe can easily be doubled—make two puddings for giving or make one for giving and one for your own table. Include a small crock or jar of Orange Rum Butter (see page 89) as part of the gift.

1 cup sifted all-purpose flour
1 teaspoon ground cinnamon
½ teaspoon grated nutmeg
½ teaspoon baking soda
¼ teaspoon salt
½ cup finely chopped suet (see Note)
½ cup dark molasses
½ cup buttermilk *or* plain yogurt
1 large egg, lightly beaten
1 cup chopped dried figs
Grated rind of 1 medium orange

1. Put a kettle of water on the stove to boil. Grease a 1½-quart pudding mold and its lid very well.

2. Into a mixing bowl, sift together the flour, spices, baking soda, and salt. Blend in the suet. In a separate bowl, combine the molasses, buttermilk, and egg and mix well. Gradually beat the dry mixture into the liquid mixture, beating until the batter is smooth. Fold in the figs and orange rind.

3. Transfer the batter to the prepared pudding mold and cover the mold tightly with its lid. (If the mold has no lid, cover the mold with a double layer of greased wax paper and tie with string. Cover the wax paper with aluminum foil.)

4. Place the mold on a rack in a large, deep pot and pour boiling water around the mold to cover its lower half. Cover the pot, place over medium heat, and steam the pudding for 2 hours, replenishing the water as needed.

5. Remove the mold from the pot, place on a wire rack, and allow to cool to room temperature. Refrigerate the pud-

ding, stored in the covered mold, for at least a week before serving; it will keep for several months.

6. To serve, allow the pudding to come to room temperature, then steam it again for 1 hour. Unmold the pudding onto a heatproof platter or cakestand and serve with whipped cream or Orange Rum Butter (recipe follows).

◆ Using wide ribbon, tie a big bow onto the handle of the lid of the mold (or remove the pudding from the mold, wrap it in cellophane, and tie up with ribbon). Tuck a sprig of holly or juniper into the bow and include instructions for rewarming and serving on the gift tag.

NOTE Suet is traditional but chilled shortening can be substituted; cut it into the flour mixture using a pastry blender or two knives.

"The wise man does not lay up treasure. The more he gives to others, the more he has for his own."

LAO-TSZE

ORANGE RUM BUTTER

Makes about 1 cup

¾ cup (1½ sticks) butter, softened
⅓ cup sifted confectioners' sugar
3 tablespoons light rum
Grated rind of 1 small orange
1 teaspoon orange juice
¼ teaspoon ground ginger
¼ teaspoon ground cinnamon
⅛ teaspoon grated nutmeg

In a small mixing bowl, beat all the ingredients together until smooth. Pack into a half-pint jar or small crock, cover, and chill.

◆ Cover the jar lid with a pinked circle of tartan fabric, tied on with a grosgrain ribbon. Include a note on the tag that the butter should be refrigerated until about 20 minutes before serving.

Hazelnut-Coconut Brittle

Makes about 1 pound

2 cups sugar
1 tablespoon butter
1 teaspoon vanilla
½ pound shelled hazelnuts, coarsely chopped and lightly toasted (see page 71)
2 cups shredded coconut, lightly toasted

1. Prepare a large baking sheet by spraying lightly with vegetable spray.

2. Place the sugar in a large, heavy saucepan over medium heat. Cook, stirring constantly, until the sugar is melted. Stir in the butter and continue cooking until the mixture is a deep amber. Remove from the heat, stir in the vanilla, then immediately stir in the hazelnuts and coconut.

3. Pour the mixture onto the prepared baking sheet and, using a narrow spatula, spread it out to a thickness of about ⅓ inch. Allow to cool completely and harden. Break the brittle into pieces and store in wax paper–lined tins.

"Christmas won't be Christmas without any presents."
LITTLE WOMEN

Apricot-Almond Snowballs

Makes approximately 4 dozen

These pretty confections make a nice after-dinner treat.

1½ cups dried apricots, coarsely chopped
1 cup golden raisins
⅓ cup Amaretto liqueur
Grated rind of 1 orange
2 cups shredded coconut
1½ cups blanched almonds, lightly toasted (see page 71)
Confectioners' sugar, for rolling

1. In the bowl of a food processor fitted with the steel chopping blade, combine all ingredients except the confectioners' sugar. Using short pulses, process until the mixture is finely chopped and well blended.

2. Place about ½ cup confectioners' sugar in a shallow bowl and lay out a large piece of wax paper on the work surface. A generous teaspoonful at a time, roll the fruit mixture into balls. Roll the balls in the sugar to coat very well and then place them on the wax paper. Let the balls stand for 1 hour before wrapping.

◆ Place each candy in a small pleated paper cup or pack the candies in single layers, with wax paper between each layer, into wax paper–lined tins. Cover tightly and store in a cool, dry place.

My Special Holiday Cordial

Makes 2 quarts

4 cups sugar
2 cups water
3 cups (1 12-ounce package) cranberries
2 cups strawberries or raspberries, fresh or frozen
Peel of 1 large orange, cut into strips
3 cinnamon sticks
1 heaping teaspoon whole cloves
1 teaspoon whole allspice
6 cups vodka

1. In a large, heavy saucepan, combine the sugar, water, berries, orange peel, and spices. Bring to a simmer and cook, covered, for 20 minutes. Strain the mixture through a double layer of cheesecloth.

2. In a large bottle or jar, combine the above mixture with the vodka. Cover tightly and store 3 to 4 weeks in a cool, dark place, shaking the container every few days.

3. Strain the liquid through a sieve lined with a double layer of cheesecloth, lightly pressing the fruit to extract as much of the juices as possible. Strain the liquid again and repeat until it's clear. Pour the liquid into two 1-quart bottles, cover tightly, and store in a cool, dark place for two weeks before using.

Wrapping It All Up

GIFT PACKAGING AND GIFT BASKETS

WRAPPING JARS AND BOTTLES FOR GIVING

◆ Look for unusual bottles and jars in kitchenware shops and gift shops. Flea markets and antiques shops are good sources for unusual old bottles and jars, too (be sure to clean them thoroughly before using).

◆ Cover jar lids with pinked circles or squares of fabric tied on with ribbons, satiny cords, brown twine, lace trim, or rickrack. Or simply tie a beautiful ribbon around the jar collars.

◆ Wrap up a whole jar with fabric and tie as above.

◆ Cover the jar lids with lacy paper doilies, secure with rubber bands, and tie as above.

◆ Tuck jars or bottles into homemade or store-bought paper bottle bags (cut down the height for short jars) and tie with twine or ribbons.

◆ Tie a decoration into the bow—a few small flowers, an herb sprig, a cinnamon stick, a cookie cutter, etc.

◆ At Christmastime, tie a few silvery jingle bells into the bow. Or tuck in a few tiny pinecones or a sprig of bittersweet, evergreen, or holly.

WRAPPING BREADS AND CAKES FOR GIVING OR SENDING

◆ Wrap breads or cakes tightly in plastic wrap, then use a linen tea towel as gift wrap. Tie up with ribbon, shiny cord, or twine and tuck a sprig of holly, bittersweet, or evergreen into the bow.

◆ Wrap in cellophane, seal with cellophane tape (old-fashioned Scotch tape), and tie with wide, shiny colorful ribbon.

◆ If a cake is large and/or delicate, before wrapping it place it on a board (select an antique or new breadboard or cutting board as part of the gift) or corrugated cardboard cut to the shape of the cake.

◆ For shipping and sending, shoe boxes, covered with decorative paper, are perfect for rectangular and oval loaves

(use children's shoe boxes for smaller loaves). Wrap the loaf well in plastic wrap and add a ribbon or other decorations and place in the box on a bed of popcorn. Surround and cover the loaf with more popcorn before putting the lid on the box and wrapping and labeling it for shipping.

Recycled Packaging

◆ Many of the containers from store-bought foods that we generally toss away without a second thought can be put back into service for packing homemade goods (note, however, that home-canned goods should be packed into proper canning jars and sealed accordingly). Here are a few of the things I use over again.

◆ *Wooden berry baskets* in pint and quart sizes are great for packing cookies: line the basket with a pretty napkin and wrap the package in cellophane. Larger produce baskets can be used for gathering several gifts together in one package.

◆ *Bottles*. Wine bottles can be reused for flavored vinegars or homemade liqueurs; seal with new corks. Bottles from imported oils and vinegars are often unusually shaped and make great containers for the homemade kind. I recycle ketchup bottles for my own Cranberry-Walnut Ketchup (page 86).

◆ *Glass jars* of all shapes and sizes are usable for just about anything, from soup to nuts.

Special Gift Baskets

Gift baskets are always nice ideas. Almost any basket will do. Decorate or wrap each item, wrap the basket in cellophane, and tie up with wide ribbon or cord. Here are just a few ideas.

- *For a tea lover*. A small tin of special tea with an English Muffin Loaf (page 12), a jar of any kind of preserves, and one beautiful antique teacup and saucer, all tucked into a basket lined with a fussy napkin.

- *For a theater lover or movie fan.* A bottle of champagne, a package of Pecan-Cashew Popcorn Balls (page 72), and a little envelope containing theater tickets or the latest videocassette film.

- *For a cook*. An assortment of unusual antique or handmade cookie cutters along with a batch of cookies made with them and a few handwritten recipe cards (or a copy of this book!), all packed into an earthenware or Depression glass mixing bowl.

- *For just about anyone*. A few jars of a variety of condiments or preserves in a small basket; include a small, ornate old silver serving spoon or a crystal jam jar, or the latest book by the recipient's favorite author.

Index